ILLUSTRATIONS
Without
SERMONS

ILLUSTRATIONS
Without
SERMONS

Bill Lufburrow

Abingdon Press/Nashville

ILLUSTRATIONS WITHOUT SERMONS

This book is printed on acid-free paper.

Library of Congress Cataloging-in-Publication Data

Lufburrow, William A.
  Illustrations without sermons.
  Includes index.
  1. Homiletical illustrations. I. Title.
BV4225.2.L83 1985 / 251'.08 / 85-13333

  ISBN 0-687-18677-3 (pbk. : alk. paper

MANUFACTURED BY THE PARTHENON PRESS AT
NASHVILLE, TENNESSEE, UNITED STATES OF AMERICA

To

DOTTIE, HOWARD, and STEVE

WHO HAVE ALWAYS
SERVED AS
ILLUSTRATIONS

Contents

ILLUSTRATIONS
Without
SERMONS

Foreword

All of us have complained about sermons without illustrations. This book is a collection of illustrations without sermons.

Like the Old Testament Book of Esther which never mentions God, this book doesn't mention God often. There are God-like thoughts, and there are God-inspired ideas, but there are only a couple of times when God is mentioned by name. The reader must supply the theology to the illustrations.

It is easy to hear sermons. Turn on a radio or television set on any Sunday morning, and the variety of messages can stagger the soul. Yet even the most careful of sermon listeners will testify that most sermons aren't very memorable. In the thousands of sermons I have heard, only a few have remained in my memory. It is not that the content wasn't good or that the preacher wasn't sincere. The problem lies not in the truth being projected, but rather in the quality of the illustrations. Most of us remember the illustrations in a good sermon, but seldom do we recall the exposition or the text. So, illustrations are essential in order to tie the good thoughts together.

Henry Lambdin was professor of homiletics while I was a student at the School of Theology at Drew University. Dr. Lambdin had long been a successful preacher, so he brought personal experience to his classes. I always eagerly attended and never failed to come away with pages of notes.

When my turn came to be the "preacher" before the class, Dr. Lambdin's analysis of my work was a combination of compliment and complaint. I shall never forget his words. He smiled, looked me straight in the eye, and said, "Lufburrow, you have an ability to use an illustration but you never say anything."

I doubt if anyone got more from Dr. Lambdin's classes than I did. If he didn't say anything else to me that year, he implanted a thought in my mind which has never left me. After two thousand speeches and visits to over two hundred pulpits across America, I've never made a speech or entered a pulpit to preach without thinking that my illustrations must say something. Sometimes I have failed and when I have, I have suffered and so has the sermon. But with the reminder of his words I have attempted to relate the illustrations and stories to some pertinent thought. The result has been that I have always tried very hard to say "something."

The thoughts in this book are designed to say something, but only when they are applied carefully by the reader or the speaker to the central theme of the user's thought process. Alone they don't "say anything." Properly applied to the situation or the time, they can inspire or illustrate. The preacher can use "license" to weave them into the message. The public speaker at the secular banquet can use them as meaningful fillers. The reader, seeking inspiration, can apply them to the process of living. All can create their own sermons.

So, the reader must supply the theology and the text to these illustrations. And the wonderful thing about God's truth is that it can be applied universally. Your particular brand of faith can be applied to these illustrations, or vice versa, because the power of good in this universe can always be illustrated the same way. Only doctrinal differences separate us. Illustrations can unite us as we search for the truth. But remember, no sermon is complete with only the illustrations. And when the theology and the text are applied, no sermon is finally complete until it is lived.

Eccentricity

A man called me "eccentric" today. They have called me all sorts of things over the years, but this is the first time I have been called eccentric.

I reached for the dictionary to check the definition. All I could think of was the old man who lived amidst his piles of newspapers, and when he died they found thousands of dollars beneath his mattress. He was eccentric! Then I read the definition. "An eccentric person deviates from the norm. An eccentric person operates away from the center."

Deviates? I always thought of a deviate as one who molests little girls, but "Mr. Webster" told me that a deviate also is one who "operates away from the norm."

I still wasn't sure if my friend had complimented or insulted me, and so as I went about my business, I did a lot of serious thinking. I really wasn't sure that I wanted the label of an eccentric deviate.

But the more I thought about it, the more I liked it. If the center, or the norm, is where the majority of the people in my world are existing, then I was perfectly satisfied with the label. The truth is that I have no desire to be like everyone else. I want to be different. The words of my mother linger in my memory. "Don't say everyone is doing it," she would tell me. "Stand tall—above the crowd," she would remind me. "I don't want you to be like everyone else," she said again and again.

Once I was called "young and impetuous" by another friend. He was excusing what he thought was a decision that I had made too quickly. I remember the occasion well, and I was hurt by his words at first, until I thought it all over. "I would rather be young and impetuous, than to be old and deliberate," I wrote to him. Youth and the compulsiveness of youth are things which leave too soon, and time provides for the opposite.

I am older now, and no one refers to me as "young" anymore, except for a few octogenarian friends. Occasionally someone alludes to some decision or action of mine with one of the synonyms of "impetuous." I never want to be so old that I fear to act.

So if youth and impetuosity and eccentricity and deviation mean that I move to get things done, I feel alive. Too many people go through life accomplishing little more than finding food, clothing, and shelter; and even then, a vast majority in the world do rather poorly at these tasks.

Few are those who are driven by a desire to change the world for individuals or groups. And few there are who listen to the beat which causes them to fear nothing in the quest for their particular brand of success. Rest peacefully, Mother! I have been "different." My peers have not pulled me aside. I have been my own man! And while I have made more mistakes than I can possibly count, the life you gave me has been filled to overflowing with successes in my chosen endeavors. If this has been because of eccentricity, I willingly accept the label.

Reflections After the Fire

The house burned down last night! Sifting through the rubble for a glimpse of yesterdays is a sobering experience. Are the trinkets which kindle memory worth grieving over . . . the pictures, the wall hangings, the classical record collection, the little gifts from friends, the borrowed books yet to be read, the antiques, the paintings, the portraits gone forever, the books, the books, the books! I sifted almost aimlessly and read cherished titles still visible through the charred remains. Then when it was over and I walked away, it was a feeling very much like the heaviness which comes as one walks from a cemetery after a graveside service.

Fortunately, it takes a while for the mind to fully comprehend the losses. As the fire department removes itself and the insurance adjuster leaves, the thoughts begin to come into focus, and some sense of reality finally arrives.

"I'm grateful for life" is the first thought. You have been saying it all day anyway! It's almost automatic as you mumble that appreciation to well-wishers and close friends. "It could have been worse!" "No hair was even singed. We are alive!" You have been saying it, and now you can really reflect on it. You really can build new houses, buy new furniture, start to assemble a new array of trinkets. How grateful we are that precious life was not wasted as the precious possessions crumbled.

Then the reality of faith returns also. The wet and charred book came apart in my hands. It was a sacred book! I had used it when I had conducted hundreds of funerals over the years, and part of the sacredness of the book were the names of those who had passed on . . . names now burned and forgotten by me. But the paper clip kept the book open to the words I have read over and over again, but which took on new meaning. "God is our refuge and strength. A very present help in trouble." As the soggy pages were returned to the rubble, I remembered assuredly that the rain and the sunshine both come to us in unexpected and equal measures. I also remembered that the real secret to life is to learn not to drown in the rain or to burn in the sunlight.

We can be grateful for life, for memories, and for the faith which brings more smiles than tears and which gives the energy to go on.

Besides, won't it be great to have the challenge of building new memories and of accumulating new hopes. We have so much to look forward to. We are alive and new!

Written in the Hospital

It is difficult to record one's thoughts and to do it accurately when health has slipped away for a time. The reaction of "denial" used to be the prominent emotion, but after a few episodes of illness repeat themselves, a feeling of pseudo discouragement takes over. I use the word "pseudo" because I find it difficult to be discouraged for very long about anything. The door opens and the chambermaid appears, and suddenly my love for human communication takes over and what was discouragement for one moment changes into gratitude in another.

Fortunately, gratitude is the feeling that lingers, and I find myself playing host to a myriad of memories and an abundance of assurances that cast the poorer thoughts to the dark and back recesses of the mind.

"How can one be discouraged," I wonder, "when life has been so full and rich and when the unknowns have been revealed in so many gentle and awesome ways, as if by some divine plan?"

Surely the Almighty is too busy to preordain these revelations, and yet the power of God which emanates from his omnipotence is sufficient to cure and not to curse —to comfort and not to condemn. The prick of a nurse's needle is not sufficient to sap the spiritual strength of one so blessed, nor is the vial of blood enough to remove the entire essence of the innermost substance of faith which causes pain to be brief, but memory to be enriching.

So I feast on memory! I actually can smell the pine trees in the New England forests. My memory permits me to hear the voices, in original tones, of loved ones who have long gone or who live on other ground. The mysterious and unexplainable mind's eye can vividly recall physical feats of varied sorts, and even the recall of a Pacific Ocean wave upon a beach brings an imaginary mist into my face.

To one who has traveled from coast to coast, city to city, on a variety of conveyances including train, plane, car, ship, and motorcycle, a short interlude of illness becomes only an inconvenience. To one who has mingled with the rich and the poor, the famous and the infamous, the holy and the unholy—who has shared experiences, conversations, and plights with men and women from all walks of life—the "slight momentary affliction" is just that . . . a temporary and insignificant time of delay. But it also becomes a time to relax and to reflect.

To reflect on the happier moments of yesterday, or even the challenges which passed by before they could be realized, would be entertaining and time consuming; but not so valuable as to spend the time in "preflection." Tomorrows are yet to unfold and more joys are to unveil themselves—unless one is content to count only the shekels of memory.

As age brings its slight infirmities, the temptation is to pause, then to rest, then to reflect, but these can become habit forming—especially when the energy of youth is not as "urging" as it has been. So one is called to seek stimulating tomorrows. The richest of all men are those who can leave this life while still in the midst of creativity, concern, thanksgiving, and service. Each new day can reveal a beauty never seen before. This very morning a storm cloud approached a vividly colored cloud which brightly carried the sun's reflection. I watched from my window to see which would win. "But what does it matter," I thought! We need the rain, but we also need the sunlight. Nature conducts its own contests, and so must we! The clouds will gather but the sunshine is never far away. The secret is to understand that they are both inevitable, even in our personal lives, and then to be able to live in the rain without drowning and in the sunlight without burning. To unlock this secret is to find the life "in abundance" which we are promised and to satisfy the predestination which God has willed for each of us.

Who?

Once I was responsible for the program at a civic club. The speaker was to be the police chief, and when a crisis developed at City Hall I was sure that the speaker would be more timely than I had imagined. Then all of a sudden he resigned and called me to cancel his speaking date.

The incident reminded me that nothing is ever final and definite. Circumstances change; events change; and so do people. Our scheduled speaker couldn't come as chief of police because he wasn't chief of police any longer. As the old saying goes, "He was just penciled in."

We're all "just penciled in"! Sooner or later all of us will experience change in life. It could be in job, marriage, or in life itself. We all move on!

The major difference in change depends on its predictability. Program chairpersons change regularly. But other changes in life are surprises. Isn't it great that we don't know what's coming? How dull—or fearful—life would be if we knew what to expect.

There's another thought which we can't fail to recognize. Most of us will not be remembered for very long after we have been erased. Only a few will find their names permanently inscribed in the pages of history. The rest will have to be satisfied with being penciled in for a short time, like Chief What's-his-name!

One in a Million

I have a friend who has a sign over his desk. It reads, "It's amazing how much you can accomplish if you don't care who gets the credit." My observation is that even this man likes to have credit for something he has done. That is, if it's something worthwhile. Most of us are quick to give someone else credit when our action isn't what it should be. That's when "credit" is referred to as "blame."

Even though my friend's sign is hard to follow, it's a good philosophy. The Bible suggests that we not let our left hand know what our right hand is doing. How tough it is!

I opened my mail a few months ago and there was a check for $1,000. It's not unusual for "my favorite

19

organization" to receive checks, but I'd never known of a cashier's check which enabled the donor to remain anonymous.

All sorts of thoughts went through my mind. I wondered why he was so secretive. Was he really that modest? Did he steal the money and was he trying to ease his conscience? "Or maybe he is trying to drive me out of my mind by making me wonder," I thought.

It's sad that an unusual act of anonymous good should start such negative thoughts, and yet that check has kept me wondering about the man and his motive ever since. I really suspect that I ran across the "one in a million" who quietly goes about doing good without any desire for recognition.

We need more folks who give of themselves, not just in the form of money, but in so many acts of kindness, encouragement, and decency. Try it today! Chances are you'll nearly burst as you keep from telling someone what you've done, but if you can really keep your good deed a secret, you'll find that "it's amazing what you can accomplish if you don't care who gets the credit."

Getting Through the Storms

I saw a picture the other day. It featured a huge sailing ship and these words: "No one cares about the storms you have encountered, but whether or not you brought in the ship."

This old adage is not totally true, of course, because most of us *like* to hear the details of our friend's exciting hunting or fishing trip, and we even like to hear the success stories of growing businesses or adventures if they aren't recited too many times.

Perhaps a change or two might be in order in revising the wording. It might be more accurate to say, "No one *listens* to the tales of storms encountered unless you *have* brought in the ship." Thereby a note of "credibility by experience" enters the picture.

Bankers lend money on what a man is going to do in the storms of the business life, but only if he has done something already. Gamblers bet more on a horse which already has been a winner. Personnel directors hire leaders only if such persons have brought in the ship and not just been in the storm. And on and on we can go with illustrations.

All of us live through storms, but it's how we weather them that counts. This is particularly true as we grow older and test our memories. Sometimes we talk too much about what we've done, and sometimes by so doing the accomplishments seem bigger than they actually were.

It behooves all of us to continue bringing in the ships. It is good for us to make a little self-examination to see if we talk more about the storms than we should. There are plenty of ships in life which won't make it unless we take hold of the wheel. Remember, "No one cares about the storms you've encountered, but whether or not you've brought in the ship."

Cheers!

A couple of weeks ago, my front door bell rang at 9:45 p.m. When I opened it, I found six or eight children ranging in ages from six to ten. Their spokesman said,

"Hi! We're cheering up the neighborhood!" Then he said, "One-two-three," and they all yelled, "Cheer! Cheer! Cheer!" They disappeared as quickly as they had arrived.

As I closed the door and returned to my chair, I was conscious of two thoughts. First, I didn't realize that the neighborhood needed "cheering up." Perhaps the kids represented homes where Dad was constantly talking about his yard. Maybe mother was unhappily married and couldn't keep that secret from the kids. Or maybe the children felt that cheer was what the neighborhood needed because they had just heard a depressing newscast on television.

I don't remember understanding much about depression and discouragement when I was a kid. To feel the need to cheer up the community was something that never crossed my mind. Life was simple but happy. If memory serves me correctly, my neighbors felt the same way.

Then the second thought I had was one of appreciation. Even though I hadn't been "down in the dumps" when the kids came to the door, I realized that I felt better than I had before. "Bless their hearts," I thought. "If they can cheer up a guy who didn't even know he needed it, they are preadolescent experts at adult psychology."

I came away from the experience with two obligations. I'm going to take a better look at my neighborhood to see where cheer is needed, and I'm going to have more faith in tomorrow's youth. And in case you haven't realized it, these thoughts were supposed to cheer you up. "Cheer! Cheer! Cheer!"

A "Frank" Statement

When I was a kid, I had a friend named Frank McGee. Frank was a few years older, and as far as I was concerned he could do no wrong. If he had taken his mother's umbrella to jump off a cliff, I would probably have hung on for the ride because I had perfect trust in Frank.

As I grew older I realized that I had to make my own decisions, and that even though Frank was a great friend, his method of life was not necessarily the one I wanted. "How foolish to have an idol," I thought.

Then as the years went by and I grew older still, I realized that everyone has an idol in another person. It seems to be a part of human nature. Every preacher looks at another and says, "Oh, if only I could preach like that." Every school teacher looks down the hall and says, "Oh, if I only could maintain discipline like she does." Every business person looks at another and says, "Now that's the kind of person I wish I could be."

It seems to stand to reason then that while you and I have secret idols, we are someone else's idol. Someone is watching us. It might be that young man in the office or in the cafeteria. It could even be one of your children.

The whole point is that we have a responsibility we might not even know about. For that reason we need to hold our heads high in dignity and in community service. We need to be above reproach in our personal and business dealings. While the world changes, we owe it to that unknown person who is watching us to remain steadfast to the idea which first caught their attention.

Roots Are Important

I'll never forget a visit with my dad several years ago! We made the usual trip to the cemetery and then drove around the "old neighborhood" so that he and I could reminisce about the old days. Dad was over eighty then, so his memory went way back, and fortunately the years did not dull his power of recall.

As we drove up and down the familiar streets, different because of the evolutionary processes of social change, we both pointed out the highlights of those days of yesteryear. A home, a vacant lot, a rock, a memory of those long gone, and then I spotted it. I spotted the tree which sat on the edge of the hill. I remember the tree well because we used to build up the snow around its rugged base and use its large "above surface" root as the jumping off place for our sleds. All around me the homes had deteriorated, but that tree with its convenient root still stood. I wondered if the kids of the neighborhood had discovered its winter value.

It was such a small thing on that afternoon with Dad, but the thrill of sled-jumping from that little hill has remained with me since it was rekindled. It was James Barrie who said, "God gave us memory that we might have roses in December." One of the most precious gifts we can have is the gift of recall. Stored within our computer brains is a wealth of information, but the amazing thing is that we usually remember the pleasant experiences before we remember the others. I hope it works that way for you!

As Dad pointed out, "We can't go back." And who really wants to? The external settings change—loved ones die, buildings crumble, and neighbors move. It seemed that everything was changed—except that tree root and the blessing of memory.

We're All Different!

Since I never took any lessons on being a parent, I've had to "play it by ear" over the years and to "call them the best way that I could." Some of my decisions with my kids were great. Some were not so hot.

I remember when my sixteen-year-old son was having problems with algebra. Part of the problem was that he had nearly given up on those equations, and part of it was that his brain just didn't function that way. Each time he discussed it with me, I saw history repeating itself.

I hated algebra! Not only did I not apply myself, I was fully convinced that I just couldn't do it. What's more, I didn't see why I'd need that stuff in the future. On that issue I guess I was right because so far no one has ever asked me if I passed or failed my algebra.

But I couldn't be that honest with my son. If I'd told him how I really felt about that difficult brand of math and how a friendly math teacher helped me through, he simply wouldn't have tried again.

One night when he sat down to tell me how frustrated and concerned he was over algebra, I wished I had had that course in how to be a parent. And when he asked what good it was going to do him in the future, I knew I couldn't tell him how I really felt, so this is what I said.

Putting on my best look of fatherly wisdom, I told him that if algebra did nothing else for him it would forever remind him that all men don't share the same talents. As he grew older, I assured him he would look at every other man with an added measure of respect because that man, rich or poor, young or old, educated or uneducated, just might be able to do algebra!

It has worked that way for me. So if you want my respect, just keep me guessing about your algebra grade, and you always will be tops in my book.

No Hatred—Please!

Some of my favorite proverbs on friendship include: "Friendship will not continue to the end which is begun for an end"; "He who turns an enemy into a friend is the bravest hero"; "Every man should have a fair-sized cemetery in which to bury the faults of his friends"; "One of the best ways to keep friendships is to return them." Then, there is this picturesque proverb: "Do not remove a fly from your friend's head with a hatchet."

Did you ever count the number of your friends? Before you read on, stop and make that count. How many did you find? Were there more than the fingers on your hands, or were there less?

These thoughts are about friends, not acquaintances. Most of us are surrounded by acquaintances, but using the classic definitions of friendship, I suspect we have a limited number of friends. It has been said that a friend is one who knows all and keeps the good, but throws the bad away.

A friend knows our weaknesses and accepts them. A friend knows our strengths and appreciates them. A friend defends us. A true friend also chastises and questions us if the occasion arises without fear of breaking the bond. A friend weeps with us and laughs with us. A friend is the first one we call to share good news and tell about bad news. A friend cares and understands.

Now, using these definitions, how many friends do you have? Or let's put it this way, are you a friend or an acquaintance of those you consider your friends?

How much richer we would be if we could turn three acquaintances into three friends each year!

Wake Up!

In the course of my work, I find myself at about one hundred head tables in the course of any year. Most crowds look the same. Take a service club for example. They really look about the same wherever they are—as a group, that is. The only thing that makes the clubs different is the individuals in it. So as I sit through endless pre-speaker ceremonies at various head tables, I select various individuals for scrutiny.

There is always one person in the crowd who becomes a challenge for the speaker because he looks as if he has been forced to attend. When you spot such a character, you usually can spot the person who forced him to attend. Sometimes you'll see a spouse nearby, or sometimes you get the idea that the strong arm has come from a boss who "requested" the person to attend. These become challenges to speakers.

Then there is the eager beaver who hurries through the meal expectantly and who perches on the edge of the seat with face tilted slightly upward so as to catch every word of the program. A speaker appreciates these appreciative persons.

A very important audience participant is the one who will laugh at each joke even if he has heard it, and usually when it's not even funny. Most speakers wouldn't make it without these assistants.

And in every audience there is one person who cannot stay awake. Usually it's caused by a late night out or advancing age, but the speaker is unnerved because he is afraid the speech has put the person to sleep. Most speakers can't keep their eyes from wandering back to the sleeper.

You don't have to visit a head table to make these observations. Next time you watch a head table, see if these observations hold. That is, if you can stay awake!!!

Symbiosis

Recently, when I asked a friend what he did for a living, he replied that he dealt in "symbiotics." I must have looked puzzled and bewildered because he immediately asked, "You do know what symbiosis is, don't you?"

My mind began to reach back to some of my "book learnin'," and it searched for a clue in theology, Greek, Latin, sociology, etc. Just as I began to recall something from a biology course from a long time ago, my friend defined the word. "Symbiosis," he said, "is the intimate living together of two kinds of organisms, especially where such association is of mutual advantage." Then he went on to explain how his specialty was uniting man and computer in harmonious relationships.

I think I was born too soon to get all wrapped up in computers as some of my younger colleagues are, but it occurred to me that even before computers came along, all of us were called on to practice "symbiosis." If there is anything we must learn to do in this complex world, it is to live together in such harmony that there is continuous mutual advantage.

It seems to me that we sometimes create mutual disadvantages because of the polarizations we establish in our everyday dealings. A word or deed or business deal that goes sour is often the cause of estrangement which is in direct conflict with symbiosis.

All of this is to suggest that we need to think of the word "symbiotics" regularly if we are to find peace.

Happy commensalism!

Music Hath Charm

What would the world be like without music! It's hard for me to imagine how Beethoven wrote his greatest works while he was deaf. It is also hard for me to imagine the loneliness which some of my deaf friends feel as they live in a world without music.

I owe my Dad a lot, but one of the greatest gifts he passed on to me was my appreciation for music. He wrote these lines about music:

When you're feeling worn and tired, and you want to be inspired, or your nervous equilibrium is shot, ponder well this declaration (for it's no exaggeration), music makes the finest tonic of the lot.

For controlling the emotions, it excels the rarest potions (not in bottles, pills, or tablets by the gross); but in melody and measure, all compounded for your pleasure—in a tasty and exhilarating dose!

Music soothes distresses faster—better than a mustard plaster—and serenely puts the shattered nerves to rest. Champion of feeling fixers, king and queen of all elixirs—it is great for getting troubles off the chest!

Would you like to taste of sadness or enjoy the thrill of gladness? Are there memories you want to call to mind? Turn your ear in the direction of a suitable selection, and observe the mystic magic you will find!

Music stirs imagination and induces relaxation. Though it's never yet been known to cure a cold, it assists in dietetics—even aids in anesthetics, and excels the best prescription ever sold.

So writes my Dad. If you need some medicine for what ails you, perhaps music can help. Happy listening!

The Crater Remains

In the town of Petersburg, Virginia, there are many reminders of the War Between the States. When I visit in the Ft. Lee area, I make it a practice to go to the battlegrounds to re-experience "The Crater."

The Crater is an indentation in the ground that has lasted over these years as a reminder of one of the most unusual military ventures of the war. The Southern forces were encamped behind a small hill, and the Northern forces were only a few hundred yards away. There was a large contingent of Union troops from the coal mines of Pennsylvania in that group, and they conceived the idea of digging a mine tunnel to an area beneath the Confederate troops. The plan was to take explosives into that underground cavern and to blow up the forces located overhead. With many setbacks and with much difficulty, these Pennsylvania miners dug. The amazing thing is that they were not detected. The fuse was lit and the men waited. Nothing happened. Two volunteers went into the tunnel to find that the fuse had broken. They repaired it, torched it again, then scampered to safety.

In the early morning hours, a loud explosion was heard. The earth lifted and men and equipment were hurled upward. Chaos broke out! Those who survived the blast scrambled up the sides of the smoldering hole. The long digging had been a success.

But no one anticipated that the thousands of Union troops who rushed to the hole to continue the battle would push one another into the crater. As the wave of men marched forward, the Southern army regrouped and fired artillery into and around the hole. Four thousand men lost their lives that day.

I won't attempt to describe my feelings as I visit that particular battleground, but I will admit to being very

30

sobered by the visit. The lessons I learn about the craters I dig and sometimes fall into are countless. The next time you are in Virginia, visit the crater. The years have softened the sides, but the "depth" of it all is still there.

Old Buzzard?

Once when my dad was eighty-four, he bemoaned the fact of his old age, and at one point in the conversation he asked, "What good is an old buzzard like me?" I guess it had been such a long time since Dad had relatives older than himself that he had forgotten everything that he felt about them. This is how I answered his question.

"An old buzzard like you," I replied, "is a very important person. You are the keeper of the treasures."

He laughed and replied, "Ha, what treasures? I don't have anything that's worth much."

Here's where you are wrong, Dad. Among the treasures you hold for me are the memories of my youth. I can recall the fun we had together, the things you taught me, the shared ideas about life. As I look at you, I think of those who were near and dear to me, and for a fleeting moment I'm reminded of them as if they too were still alive . . . as you are alive. I appreciate that reminder.

Another treasure you hold is a key to my own youth. As long as you are living, Dad, I can still be the son and not the "elder." Somehow, by the magic of your presence I can fool myself into thinking that I'm not growing older. As I fool myself this way, I can still enjoy the luxury of youthful pursuits. When you are gone, I'll be expected to fall into the more sedate role of moving with the precision and dignity of a senior citizen . . . but I'm not ready for that.

Then there's one more thing, Dad, which makes it important for you to go on and on for as long as you can. A man's father is the only one who really cares about his successes and his failures. He is the only one who can see the mistakes and still say, "That's my boy." And that's worth a whole lot!

What do you mean, "What good is an old buzzard like me?" That's a silly question. Pay attention, Pop! We love you because you hold these treasures . . . and a whole lot more! I hope he's listening!

* * * * * * * * * *

"This business of dying is not so bad. It's getting ready that's difficult."—(Dad, the week before he died.)

Fences

I'm very conscious of fences these days. Three years ago I labored over a long split rail fence in the back of my home, and I have shown the fence to everyone who would look. A couple of acres of woods formed a natural backdrop for the fence. A few weeks ago I went home from work only to find that a new neighbor had purchased the ground and immediately backed my prized split rail fence with a six-foot cedar fence. It doesn't take much imagination to know that my fence had to come down.

The next weekend I dug, pulled, lifted, and dug some more until all that now remains of my rustic fence is a pile of split rails and some heavy posts. My only comfort is that the neighbor's new fence will undoubtedly keep out the armadillos—at least from that direction.

Taking down a fence is not only good physical exercise, but can become a time for philosophical exercise as well.

It occurred to me that man builds three types of fences. The first type is designed to keep something in. Prison fences exist for that purpose. Yard fences are sometimes used to keep pets within the confines of the yard.

The second type of fence we build is designed to keep something out. The old castle walls were built to deter the invading armies. The fences around apartment parking areas are there to keep the car thieves out.

The third type of fence we build is a decorative fence. It complements the area on both sides.

I'd really like to know whether my new neighbor built his fence to keep his dog in or me out. And as we go through life building fences around ourselves, it would behoove us to really examine the "fences" we build. Are they to keep ourselves and our ideas and our possessions in because we think they are best, or do we build them to keep others out so that they do not invade whatever solitude is ours?

I suggest that to live in the real world one must realize that only decorative fences are the super goal for mankind. As we interact, the utopia for which we strive has only fences which enhance and beautify both sides.

Which Line Are You In?

During a recent political discussion, I heard a man say, "When the chips are down, you can count on the conservatives to stand for what is right." I pondered that comment for some time, because it just doesn't work out that way. The moral response to what is right or wrong cannot be predicted by using a man's political feelings as a guideline.

History has shown us that regardless of where folks stand on the political spectrum, whether it is far right or far left, they are still merely human beings who are controlled by many more factors than their political position. To say that any one political party or any political view held by any American is enough to guarantee his moral integrity is to ignore the good people on both sides of the fence.

If you will look deep enough and be honest as you do, you will find that most of us are motivated by what affects us personally. We respond as we do, partly, because of environmental experience coupled with hereditary make-up, but mostly we act from emotion which is selfishly motivated. For example, the benefits from the income tax laws make us more generous. The expectation of a returned kindness motivates us to be more gentle. The promise of rewards causes us to work harder, and in anticipation of "stars in our crown" we become more religious.

If it could be as simple as to line up the "good people" on one side and the "bad people" on the other side, I believe we could solve the wrongs in the world very quickly. But political lines will never be drawn with such ease.

What really motivates us personally is a study which all of us need to conduct. Since we already know what is morally sound, a genuine understanding of ourselves will help to do what is right—regardless of our politics. And a sober self-evaluation might really surprise us. We just might be on the other side and haven't realized it.

Still Waving in the Breeze

As a boy growing up in Baltimore, I used to go to Fort McHenry on occasion. You will recall that the fort is at the entrance to Baltimore Harbor, and it was during the War of 1812 when it became famous. Historians tell us that Francis Scott Key, who was out in the harbor on a ship, spent the night looking for the American flag on Fort McHenry's flagpole. When he saw it still flying, he penned the words of our National Anthem.

When our schoolteachers took us to the fort, they always emphasized the location of the ship. They would stand near the waterfront and speculate on the exact spot. I remember that I was not as interested in the location of Mr. Key as I was in his words. In my imagination I could hear the shell fire and smell the gun powder, and if I closed my eyes, I could even see the stars and stripes waving in the early morning breeze. I could hear old Francis speaking to me through the years of time. "O say! Can you see? Look, there in the dawn's early light. That same flag that we hailed in the twilight's last gleaming. Look at her broad stripes and bright stars. She has lasted through the perilous night. She's still there." What a thrill it must have been for that patriot, as he was assured that the nation was still intact.

We are being reminded to look at our country through her history. But where you stand—where the ship is located—isn't really important. The important thing is that she is still a great nation, in spite of the perils she has experienced.

Wait! Listen! Can you hear Francis Scott Key? I hear him again! "O say, does the Star Spangled Banner yet wave o'er the land of the free and the home of the brave?" Yes, Francis. It still does—so far!

He Sleeps

We have an old white dog in our home. When we saw him at the SPCA, we decided to adopt him because he was so ugly we were certain that he'd be overlooked. His adoption was the best "dog-gone" decision we've ever made. He's a great companion, and when times get tough and I feel that no one loves me, old Scruffy is as loyal as a friend can be.

His major fault is that he sleeps his life away. He goes into such deep sleep on occasion that he misses the finer things in life. If we go to the kitchen for a late-night snack, he doesn't know it because he's asleep. He's so relaxed that a burglar could hold us at gunpoint, and Scruffy would sleep through it all.

Scruffy's base instincts call for sleeping. He reminds me of a lot of folks I've met over the years. You've known them too. They are the slow starters of life. They remain in the ranks of the unchallenged. They literally sleep their lives away. They follow their lowest instincts instead of responding to their highest challenges.

There is a danger which all of us face as we grow older. If we are not careful, we will lose sight of the dreams which dominated our lives in our youth. And if we're not careful, we'll assume that burglars are for someone else to pursue.

It's OK for a spoiled dog to sleep through it all, but the rest of us are expected to be stimulated by higher challenges. I wish I could convince my dog of that truth . . . and some of my friends too. But alas, I've given up on Scruffy. Maybe there is hope for the rest of us.

Regret!

A few years ago, a young auditor visited our office to conduct our yearly audit. He was a quiet young man—almost to the point of shyness—so I wouldn't believe it when a complaint came that he had kissed one of the young ladies in the office against her will. In fact, he had reportedly shut the door, turned off the light, and then kissed her. Of course, the complaints that came from her family were very embarrassing.

Feeling quite certain that this meek little man, representing a respected profession, couldn't possibly be guilty, I called him into my office and gently informed him of the complaints. Imagine my surprise when he lowered his head and admitted, "I've regretted the incident—ever since it occurred!"

I've chuckled over the whole thing on several occasions, but his words have stuck with me. "I've regretted the incident—ever since it occurred" has been a phrase that all of us have uttered at one time or another, and if we haven't, we should have! Perhaps our "crimes" haven't been as bold as to risk an unwanted kiss in the dark, but certainly we should have regretted some of our deeds.

It's so easy to stand in judgment of other persons simply because our deeds have been different or because, unlike the young auditor, we never got caught.

On that occasion, I wasn't ready to believe until he admitted that the rumors were true. Other times I've been ready to judge and to condemn just on the basis of suspicion.

If you are guilty of such prejudgment and condemnation, maybe you now feel as I do. "I've regretted the incident—ever since it occurred!"

Armadillos

I have armadillos! Some people have chinch bugs or brown patch, but I have armadillos. Judging from the extent of the damage to my lawn and gardens, I must have a whole flock . . . covey . . . herd . . . bunch, well anyway, there are a lot of armadillos in my yard.

The experts tell me that there is no way to get rid of armadillos except to catch them and take them further out in the country or to shoot them. The trouble with both of these solutions is that I never see them. They seem to know when we are not at home and when we return, even from short trips to the grocery store, we can see evidence of their visit.

Armadillos remind me of many of the social ills which plague our society. When we aren't watching, these problems creep up on us and before we know it some segment of the population has been ruined or some new regulatory agency has been created to upset the status quo. Just as the armadillos dip into the beauty of my lawn and gardens, these social poisons rip into life and destroy our peace and tranquility.

Commentators from my discipline tell us that we live in changing times and that our liberties and freedoms are threatened on every side. It doesn't take a very high-powered mind to diagnose the ills of society. The really significant persons are the folks who are prescribing the corrective answers.

Which are you? Are you finding any solutions to the world's problems, or are you only observing the decay? If you are a problem-solver, I hope you also will find the solution to my armadillos.

Jogging, Anyone?

As I go to work in the morning, I notice some of my neighbors as they run through the streets. Judging from their costumes and their gaits, they obviously are engaged in a program of jogging. I'm always a bit embarrassed when I see them, and the embarrassment is not always for me because of my own need to jog. I'm embarrassed for them!

If joggers knew how silly they looked, they would confine their activities to their backyards. The main thing that bothers me—no, amuses me—is the look on their faces. Did you ever see a jogger who looked happy? They have a certain "pained" expression on their faces which doesn't resemble anything I've ever seen before. It's a combination of hearing bad news on the stock-market report and biting into a piece of bad asparagus. It's a face that convinces me that jogging must be an unusually painful experience.

We show a lot by our faces! We don't have to be jogging to let the passersby know how we feel.

All of this is to say that we can't help the face that God gave us, but that we can practice the art of developing smiles, comforting looks, and sympathetic glances as we "jog" along through life. We can help folks by the way we look at them. And if the task makes this impossible, better quit the task—even if it's jogging.

Look for the Gardens

Outside my office window there is a beautiful garden. Actually, that garden is one of the most beautiful spots in the area. Just beyond the wrought-iron fence is a busy thoroughfare which is filled with cars, buses, and trucks of all sizes.

I have purposely watched the passersby as they go up and down the street to see if they ever glance at the garden. Even those who pass on foot, and there are many, never seem to see it. Once in awhile someone will pause and look in at the flowers, but seldom do folks turn their heads.

What is the matter with us? Are we so busy with the perplexities of modern living that we fail to pause long enough to "smell the roses," or to look in at them, as the case may be? Does it take a vacation in the mountains to get us to pause long enough to breathe the fresh air or to be inspired by the view? Is it possible that folks are so used to the clamor that is found in the inner city that they fail to recognize what beauty there is?

I think the whole problem is symbolic of our times. Over-crowding and noise and pollution of one sort or another just might deaden our desire for beauty, unless we prepare ourselves for that beauty by traveling to find it.

Since I have noticed the folks passing by and never looking, I have tried to find the beauty in every city block. I have been seeing things I've never noticed before.

I think I might even see my own garden if I passed by. Would you? Try looking at the city block you pass and see what you can find. You might be surprised!

I Forgot

A few weeks ago a friend of mine was singing a magnificent number to enhance our civic-club meeting, and he forgot his lines. With grace and ease, and with seemingly no embarrassment, he walked over to the piano and refreshed his memory. Some chuckled nervously for him; some applauded to register their understanding; some just ached for him. I was one of those. I've been there!

I'm not a singer, so I've never forgotten my lines while singing. But I have forgotten my lines while addressing an audience. In fact, it has happened more times than I want to remember. Usually a line of a poem slips my mind, and I stumble through with words that don't rhyme. Sometimes it's the punch line of a joke, and I try to fix it with something which isn't a bit funny. My friend had the right approach when he admitted his problem, corrected it, and then went on with the song.

How many times we forget our lines. It doesn't have to be as a speaker or a singer. Sometimes it can be as a salesman; sometimes as a husband or father; sometimes as a citizen or just as a human being. And the lines we forget are usually well fixed in our minds. We simply forget them. They range all the way from the magic words we are taught as children—"please" and "thank you"— to the more sophisticated words which responsible adults need to say to one another. Think a minute! Is there some line you need to speak which has seemingly left your memory? Try "I love you." Try it today!

The singer taught us a lesson that day. He admitted his mistake, corrected it, and went on! His song was so inspiring, and he sang it so well that everyone forgot that he had lost his lines. I was the only one who remembered.

I'm Cold Enough Already

I've always been fascinated by the fairly new science of cryogenics. That's the process which is used in freezing, and it's what folks are talking about when they are arranging to have their bodies frozen after death. They do it with the firm conviction that medical science will progress to a point where it will be able to cure what killed them and bring their bodies back to life.

Frankly, I have some doubts! I'm not so bold as to state that it won't ever be possible because I've been surprised too many times already. I'm just not sure if I want to come back. I think you really need to evolve with life to appreciate it. That is what constitutes wisdom. You just can't acquire it without being awake most of the time.

Can you imagine how difficult it would be for someone like Benjamin Franklin to return today after being frozen all those years. He probably would die again just from the shock of what he would find here. Just the simple task of getting around on the modern roads and freeways would take his breath. And how frustrating it would be to try to explain the cathode tube which brings pictures into our homes. And the computer would really throw him. Being a lawyer of sorts, he probably would be shocked at the changes he would find in our legal system. No, please don't freeze me when I die. Besides, I'm not sure the world could stand me twice.

This freezing idea confuses me too. Recently I had a small growth on my arm frozen with a blast of liquid nitrogen. It got all puffy and finally fell off as the doctor predicted. Won't it be a shock when they bring out all those old bodies only to have their arms and legs puff up and fall off.

And some even predicted we would never get to the moon.

Age Attainment

For the past ten years the premium on a supplemental group hospital policy I hold has been fixed in my memory. So I was startled when the bill came in with a sizeable increase. The asterisk directed me to the bottom of the invoice where I read, "Premium increased due to attained age." OUCH!

My first reaction was to pay it and to chalk it up to "one of the facts of life." Considering the alternatives I realized that growing older wasn't really so bad after all. But the more I thought about it, the more that word "attained" bothered me. I had always thought of an attainment as some good accomplished—something special that came as a result of diligent effort. I just couldn't be comfortable with the word being used as a part of an explanation for higher premium. Had the message read, "Due to advanced age" or "Because you're growing older," I could have understood, but an attainment . . . ! I couldn't accept it!

The more I thought about it, the more puzzled I became, and then I checked with Webster. "To attain," I read, is "to reach, as an end." Reading more, I saw that "attainment" means "to come to an end of progression." And believe it or not, the example used in the dictionary was "to attain a ripe old age." Birthdays I don't mind, but from now on I will mind them since I have to attach the "ripe old age" phrase to my celebration. Once more it seems to be an attainment which is irreversible.

I went to the typewriter to send a note to the insurance company. "Try another word," I suggested. "Break the news more gently," I wrote. "Don't tell a man he is in a new age bracket and try to make it seem like an achievement," I told them.

My wife read the letter, then chided, "Come on, Bill! If

you haven't noticed, the rest of us have." So I tore up the letter, paid the increased premium, and settled back to enjoy my "attainment." Ripe old age or not, it's great to be alive!

It's Gone

Admittedly I was breaking the speed limit when it occurred, so I am sure that someone will say, "Serves him right." We were going near seventy on the interstate. Only our headlights broke the darkness. No one else was around.

The car radio was fading in and out, so I put my hand out the window to raise the antenna. The wind whipped at my hand, and before I knew it my watch was blown from my wrist. There was no way I could find it, so I drove on, but I was sick at heart. It was a good watch and kept perfect time. Then, with a careless gesture, it was gone.

For the rest of the evening I was miserable. I had not only lost a valuable watch, but it had been a gift. The radio reception was improved, but I didn't want to listen, so I turned it off. How stupid of me to lose a watch so carelessly. I vowed that it would never happen again.

The more I thought about it, the worse I felt. I know all those good thoughts about "Not crying over spilled milk," "What's done is done," and all of these came to mind. But they didn't help a bit. If I could have, I would have kicked myself.

I thought of other things I had thrown away through careless acts. Heading the list would be words I let escape without thinking. Most of these things can't ever be replaced, but fortunately I can buy a new watch.

Wearing Well

Women often are accused of having clothes to fit their personalities. One lady in our office occasionally wears a particular dress, and when you see it you know it is going to be a tough day.

But men do the same thing! Well, I do anyway! In my closet are clothes I wear for the occasion. When I have an appointment to seek someone's support of a project, I reach for my pin-stripe suit. When I am going to lecture a group of young people, the coat never matches the pants. I have a suit I wear to funerals, and I have a suit I wear to western parties.

Who are we kidding anyway? "Clothes make the man (person)" up to a point, but what really counts is conversation. We can stand around a sports banquet and look all sporty, but we will be standing alone if we don't know where Pete Rose used to work. And even your funeral suit won't do any good if you don't have a note of sincerity in your voice when you say, "I'm sorry."

Conversation is important, but so many times we simply don't know what to say. Here are a couple of thoughts for next time you are at a loss for words. Try leading the conversation to the interests of the other person and not just to your own. Let the other person tell you what is important! And if you don't know anything about the subject, admit it by asking questions.

I'm convinced that if we let the other person do most of the talking, we will become known as good conversationalists. And if we remember to talk only about those things we really know, we will get home sooner.

It's not what you wear, but what you say (or don't say) that counts.

The Elegy

Not far west of the city of London is the little village of Stoke Poges. In Stoke Poges you will find "the country churchyard" which was the site of Thomas Gray's "Elegy Written in a Country Churchyard." He was probably about thirty when he finished the famous elegy, and that would have been around the year 1746.

Stoke Poges is "far from the madding crowd" (a line from the elegy), and the spot is about as quiet and peaceful as any I know. England's National Trust cares for the shrine, and even has cattle in the field next to the cemetery so that one can picture "the lowing herd . . . o'er the lea." And you might even hear a "moping owl . . . complain" as the poet did years ago.

History tells us that old Tom Gray was not really very successful as a literary genius. He only earned a total of forty guineas from his writings in his whole lifetime. In fact, they say he was just quiet and shy and spent most of his life occupying rooms at Cambridge University. Unsuccessful though he might have been, most of us can easily quote his words,

> Full many a gem of purest ray serene,
> The dark unfathomed caves of ocean bear;
> full many a flower was born to blush unseen,
> and waste its sweetness on the desert air.

In all of our twentieth-century success, we will do well if we will be remembered for two-hundred years. Most of us will be forgotten the next week. So if you are in London, be sure to visit Stoke Poges. And if you aren't planning to go, at least read the elegy. It's good for the soul!

Save the Postage

Folks are making millions as they attempt to help us solve our problems. Seminars abound! Books are plentiful. We have a variety of experts to choose from as we attempt to improve our condition.

Some of us work on solving our problems in other ways. Frankly, I like the Joseph Mobutu method of problem-solving. You will recall that he was one of the rulers in the Congo years ago. Some college students were rioting, and he solved the problem by closing the college and drafting the three thousand rioters. What a man!

We really shouldn't refer to the method as the Mobutu Method. Let's try another name, such as "Do It Now and Do It Without Thinking Approach"; or maybe it could be called the "However You Feel at the Moment Approach." How about the "Whammo Approach" to problem-solving?

Here's how it works. Your wife or husband spends too much money at the department store! Use the Whammo Approach. Burn the credit cards with the dinner candles next time you have guests. Or if your son has damaged the car three times in a row, use the Whammo Approach. Simply go out and hammer nails into all of the tires. That will stop him! Or when your secretary misspells a word, use the Whammo Approach. Simply throw a dictionary at her when she leaves tonight.

Absurd you say? Think about it for a minute! Isn't the Mobutu/Whammo Approach the one we use sometimes? It does make us feel better for a time, but how silly we feel later on. That's why some of us, who are prone to Whammos, write letters and then wait until tomorrow to send them. We save a lot of postage that way!

Show Me

Most of us wouldn't think of buying a new suit of clothes without trying it on in front of a mirror. We need to test it a bit to see how it fits us. Or to put it more properly, we need to see how it "suits us." And yet we'll buy all sorts of ideas and philosophies without trying them on first.

I've often said that in matters of politics and religion people will believe almost anything. Just turn on the radio or the television and catch some of the ideamongers as they sell their products. Someone must be buying or they wouldn't stay on the air. And some of the ideas they sell seem so bizarre. Yet night after night and day after day all forms of propaganda are sent our way in all sorts of packages. Like it or not, we are influenced. But are we standing in front of proverbial mirrors to see how these ideas really fit?

I'm not from Missouri, but I do have a "show me" attitude. I simply cannot and will not accept a philosophy just because the proponent is a good salesperson. I insist on "standing in front of the mirror and trying it on first." I insist on a "good fit" before I take a stand on any issue.

All this doesn't stop me from listening, however, so if you have a favorite subject you think I should know about, I'll be glad to look it over. And because a new suit always looks better than an old one, I might even buy your idea. Goodness knows, I can stand improvement. How about you?

Living Antiques

Two elderly sisters decided to pool their resources and move into a house by the side of the road. They enjoyed one another's company, but soon knew that they were lonely and without many friends. So they decided to change things. They put a simple sign in the front yard which read "Antiques." Soon they were visited by a man and his wife who were traveling the area to find bargains. The two sisters invited them in and gave them tea and cookies with lots of conversation. The man finally looked at his watch and asked, "Where are the antiques?" One of the sisters replied, "You're looking at them."

It was one way to get rid of loneliness, but it was also a good way to express a sense of humor. I admire anyone who continues to cultivate a sense of humor into old age.

Too many times we think of elderly people as chronic complainers or dull storytellers. All of us have been around folks who are ready to tell us about the good old days, and who are ready to recite the details of their aches and pains. "If he has told us of his gout once, he has told us about it a hundred times," we are apt to say.

An old guy who can continue to sparkle with amusement over the things around him will be a lot easier to live with and a lot more fun to remember than the old grouch so many of us are destined to become.

Cultivating the smiling disposition is something we need to work on early in life. And unless we want to be remembered as cranks, it would be wise to start now before it is too late. And by the way, forty-five is now considered as the start of being elderly. Do you want to hear about my aches? Since I'm well over the age, I have a long list.

A Risk of Rejection

A group of businesspersons were discussing an effort to "get more members." Someone suggested that each committee member should be personally responsible for three newcomers. Individuals squirmed as they thought of the added work. All agreed that the personal approach was a good idea, but no one wanted the added pressure of a formal campaign.

Then one member summed it up. He said, "The trouble with us around this table is that we aren't used to being rejected, and so no one will take that risk!"

I wanted to believe that time restraints kept me from volunteering, but maybe it was because I don't like to take the chance of rejection.

It's not that I'm not rejected occasionally. That seems to go with my kind of job. But it's a bit like cheating on a diet. I'll slip if the food is good, but I won't take the extra calories if the taste really isn't worth the consequences.

The risk of turndown didn't bother me as much as wasting a turndown on a project that wasn't my top priority.

We might do well to analyze consequences each time we risk a negative. Is it really worth it? Are we really willing to take the chance on a particular project even though life itself is full of chances? It would probably clean up the world's moral climate if we weighed the worth of the consequences before acting.

So I guess I will have to reconsider the committee assignment—either take the risk of rejection or get off the committee. And if I take the risk, and sign up a few more members . . . well, like most successes the price I have paid will be well worth it.

A Change Might Help

Have you ever noticed how many of your friends have put an addition on their home? Garages are closed in or a new fireplace is added, and sometimes the whole basic plan of the house is changed. I have often wondered what possesses us to go to the trouble, the expense, and the mess to change our living environments. Are we not satisfied with anything? Surely we knew the limitations of our homes when we moved in.

What's more, we are one of the few countries in the world where this remodeling is done so frequently. Europe, for example, is filled with homes which have never been changed for centuries. No one would want to take the responsibility to change that bit of history which can still be enjoyed in its original form. That's not the case in America, however. We never seem to be satisfied with the original creation of architect and builder.

Personally, I think it has something to do with "the American Dream." From its beginning this nation was an experiment in change, and change always has been a part of our social and political situation. Our forefathers simply weren't happy with a monarchy which had become as much of a tradition as a ruling power.

Change is good for us, and since our places of residence are often extensions of our personalities, it becomes a public admission that we are not satisfied with the status quo—that we want to change and hopefully to improve.

It was Cicero who reportedly said, "He stayed the same as before but the same is no longer befitting." He was right you know! In fact, that's what my wife tells me each time she buys a new dress. So if you have been waiting for an addition to improve your life, now is the time. Cicero said so!

Let Us Pray

A couple of the airlines still provide a prayer card on the meal tray. I was surprised and pleased that the tradition had lasted into our day and age. On a recent trip, I took special notice of the card hidden carefully under my salad plate. On the outside it read, "For those of all faiths who want to have a grace at mealtime." Inside were two selections from the Psalms.

I realized immediately that the card had been prepared by the public relations department and not by a larger committee of clergymen from "all faiths." The public-relations person was obviously from the Judeo-Christian tradition and assumed that everyone else was also. If the airline really wanted to reach "all faiths," it would take more than two Psalms to do it. Such a prayer card probably would resemble the *Airline Guide* or maybe even the Houston telephone directory.

Before I ate, I read the Psalms and they were very appropriate for me. But of course I came from the Judeo-Christian tradition too, and I like Psalms. I wondered about the passengers who were not a part of the limited "all faiths" category. In a day and age when planes are filled with persons from all over the world, I wondered about that card.

Then I decided to take a silent survey. I left my seat and wandered up and down the aisle looking at the trays. Each prayer card seemed to be undisturbed. Only one person was holding the card. It was in the hand of an elderly lady. I won't try to speculate as to whether she belonged to "all faiths."

It seemed to me that we create problems when we blindly continue to create minorities. In a place like an airplane, when all of us enter a unique fellowship of common experience, we could do without reminders of our differences.

Admittedly, you would have to pick up the card before you would be reminded of the difference. I wonder if the old lady thought about that.

Me? I needed the card too! I already knew those two Psalms from memory, but they reminded me to be thankful. Do you need the card?

Hooray for Hilltops

The next time you drive back from Austin, Texas, try the road from Paige to Smithville. It's about eighteen miles out of the way, but it's worth the ride. As you drive along over some gently rolling hills, you suddenly will come on one of the prettiest hilltops in Texas. When you least expect it, the view becomes dramatically panoramic, and if you aren't expecting it at all, you might have to catch your breath from the sight. If you don't happen to live in Texas, you can find a similar road near your home.

Recently, I went in search of that hilltop again, and as I thought about it, I remembered other favorite high spots. One is located in West Virginia. Another is in Oregon. Still another is across the bay from San Francisco. Even standing atop one of New York's skyscrapers gives me a thrill.

Probably, with the exception of those who suffer from acrophobia, most of us like hilltops. There is something majestic about the feeling one gets when one is able to survey the scene from the top. A rural real-estate salesman once told me that "everyone wants a hilltop, but no one wants to pay the price." Of course he was commenting on the cost of a choice homesite on top of the hill, but his words have stuck with me.

The price of being on top is expensive. Whether it is paying the cost of admission to view the city from a sky-scraper or reaching the top in a vocation, the price is high. Achievers never mind the cost! They keep climbing! They work hard and spend dollars, time, and effort in reaching the peak. Then if they are smart, they will pause to reflect on the climb as well as on the view from the summit.

I know many who are on top of the hill. And most of them would pay the price all over again to be there. Unless you suffer from "success acrophobia," you have to admit that the hills are better than swamps.

Tombstones

"How do you want to he remembered?" One of the senators asked that question of Judge O'Conner during the confirmation hearings for her Supreme Court appointment. She paused and then cleverly answered, "Here lies a good judge." How would you have answered that question?

The news commentator suggested that the lady was flippant in her answer, but think about that for a minute. Perhaps it was her best response all day. It was a bit evasive even if it wasn't flippant.

Judge O'Conner must have known that it is impossible for an active person to sum up a life's desire in one sentence. As a wife she must have ideals and goals. As a lawyer she certainly has a special set of standards to live up to. The same could be said for her role as a parent, friend, human being, and American citizen. In each of these categories such a well-rounded person would have need of a separate way to be remembered.

Is it enough to put on your tombstone, "Here lies a good person"? Or will they say that about you? And how have you done with your chosen vocation? Can they say, "Here lies a good citizen"? Or how about as a parent? Will they refer to that when you are remembered?

There was once a king, so the fable goes, who played dead and lay in his coffin so that he could hear what folks said about him. That's a sobering thought, and I'm not sure I really want to know. The big question is whether the mourners' opinions will match your own self-estimate.

As for me, I'm not even going to try to guess how I might be remembered, if indeed anyone remembers at all. I think I'll just borrow the epitaph I found in a Boston graveyard. It read, "I told you I was sick."

Can I Touch You?

I read *The Wall Street Journal* faithfully. My reasons probably are not the same as yours. I'm just a "poor old country preacher," and what the stock market is doing doesn't directly affect my blood pressure at all. I read the *Journal* so that I know what you are reading. I like it that way.

The cartoon and the verses on the editorial page are the best. It seems that the cartoon is always speaking to me directly. I see myself in one of the characters almost every day. Sometimes I see more of me than I want to see. The editorial and book reviews are also my favorites. If we could just get those guys in the Kremlin to believe those editorials!

I read the rest of the pages too, but then I glance over the "want ad" section. I look over those job offers and wonder if they are real. I'm especially fascinated by the overseas offers and their fringe benefits. If you let your imagination take over, reading about these jobs is a better "wish experience" than reading a travel guide or even a fancy store catalog. Can you imagine the fun of being president of a "company with unlimited growth opportunities"? The majority of the ads would have you convinced that these jobs had no problems at all, just fringe benefits.

But the part I like the best is the section on real estate. Some of my friends buy their summer homes in that section, or would like one to think that they do. This is where I see the separation between the men and the boys, the sheep and the goats. Are there really people out there who can afford those homes? Oh well, we can't all be rich.

I'll keep reading *The Wall Street Journal.* It's a great paper, and I wouldn't trade it for anything. But if any of you happen to buy one of those exotic homes, would you at least tell me about it so I could touch you?

Home Is . . . !

A friend of mine from Texas is living in West Virginia. He dreams of returning to Texas, and I know a West Virginian who works in Texas and who can't wait to retire so he can go home.

There is something about "home" that pulls and tugs at us. Not all of us want to live in the place of our roots, but most of us feel at home when we go back. I'm looking forward to my high-school reunion next year. Our class faithfully holds one every five years, and it's fun to watch the rest of them age. But it's also a good experience to be back home.

Sociologists haven't had many years to study these rather new "homesick feelings." As we emerge from a largely rural to an urban society, and as air travel makes it so easy to cover long distances in a short time, we find excuses to wander farther and farther away from the places of our birth. Not many years ago we married neighbors, and we lived right where we had always been. Only those who had lots of time and money ever got very far from home. And most of them returned to the home place eventually, if only for their own funerals. There are some who have introduced the theory that to return to the familiar spots of childhood can keep us healthy of mind. By that theory, those who never leave should be in great shape. But what about those who never go back?

I don't know about the theories, but I do know that a return to the old neighborhood is good for my soul. As I drive past the old house, I can see my mother standing on the porch, and I can hear her voice calling me for dinner. And for a few moments, I regain my youth, my strength, my innocence, and my freedom. Then instantly it fades, and I'm back in the world where I really live. I like it here. I wouldn't want to go back for more than a visit to yesteryear. Would you?

Good Old Mickey Mouse

Recently I had the occasion to be in Southern California, and when I'm there I always try to set aside some time to visit Disneyland. Some of my friends are bound to make some interesting comments as they read this, but I confess that I still get excited about Mickey Mouse and all that surrounds him. I have my favorite parts of the park, and I always head right for those areas first.

You can call me "Goofy" if you like, but let me tell you why I enjoy Disneyland. I enjoy it because I really believe that life was intended to be a happy place. In fact, life is, whether you see it or not, a magic kingdom.

Now please don't remind me that investors are getting rich on my visits to Disneyland. I know that, and I'm glad of it. That's a part of our great private enterprise system. But when I've paid for my ticket and contributed to their wealth, I enjoy the happiness I see around me. There are smiles everywhere, and I see children and adults enjoying the excitement of that unreal world.

Something always happens to me when I leave Disneyland. I come away thinking that all of life is like that. I look for smiling faces and for magic miracles taking place right before my eyes. And for a time anyway, until I'm reminded of the daily grind, I think of happiness and joy.

The older I get, the more I realize that life really can be like Disneyland. Well—the potential is there anyway. It's the people who mess it up!

In Response to Citizenship

Here I am on jury duty . . . criminal jury no less. And I don't even like criminals! Some time in the jury selection room is always an experience, and about the only thing that cheers me on is the fact that this is a responsibility of citizenship in a judicial system which I wouldn't want to trade with any other nation. But the time I'm wasting—good grief—the time!

My first thought as I look around the crowded room is which one of my fellow selectees I would want to represent me if I would happen to be on trial. That conservative-looking businessman with the bald head wouldn't be the one I would choose. I can tell by looking at him that he doesn't like criminals either. Then there is that sweet looking old housewife-type nearby. She seems to be enjoying this day out so much, I don't think I would want her on my jury because she just might try to prolong it. That overaged hippie in front of me I would not choose either. His occasional glance already tells me that he doesn't like me. Since I can't find anyone to be on my jury, I resolve not to commit the crime, so I turn my thoughts away from jury selections.

What this place needs is an efficiency expert. Is there no human concern in this world anymore? Maybe if they just painted the room some imaginative colors it would help. The impersonality of it all is killing me. Don't the folks in charge ever smile?

Here comes the judge! I recognize him anyway. And he introduces a smile, a clear voice, and an organized explanation to this whole thing. As he sits there listening to excuses from a long line of folks who want out, he resembles a priest listening to confessions. I'll bet he hears some good ones! He looks great sitting up there in all his dignity, but you would think that the county fathers could afford to put the flags back on those poles. The eagles are perched atop each pole, but not a flag adorns the bench.

Hooray for the privilege to serve! I hope I get a crack at those criminals before the day is over.

Was I chosen? Well, they haven't called me yet. It's still too early in the day for me to say anything but "Hooray for the system." Whoops! I spoke too soon. Here I go!

Denial? Not Always!

The doctor used the word "denial." When he asked the patient how he was doing, the patient replied, "Great." The doctor mumbled, "Denial."

"What did you say?" the patient asked.

"Denial," the doctor replied.

As the patient left the doctor's office, he chuckled about the word he had heard so often. It is a popular word and certainly fits some patients to be sure. The person who won't take his medicine because it is too much trouble, or the one who would rather die than have surgery is exhibiting denial, and it must be frustrating to the doctor as he attempts to do his duty. I knew a lady who was so good at it that she denied that the lump in her breast was important, and in a few months she was gone. Denial can be dangerous!

The antonym of "denial" is "acceptance." Of course the doctor wants the patient to accept the problem, to accept the diagnosis, and to accept the treatment. It's easier that way. But I submit that the word acceptance can be applied to the very necessary positive thoughts that also help in recovery. When the patient was asked how he was doing, the doctor might have been happier if the patient had moaned or groaned or complained. After all, the complaints drive the patient to the doctor in the first place.

But there are some patients who can accept the condition with such a positive noncomplaining approach that they feel better and make everyone around them feel better.

Denial? Nuts! Sometimes it's called positive thinking, and it contributes to the recovery. Or at least it makes the condition bearable. How do I feel? Great!

Me? Asleep? Never!

Fortunately I don't get tired very easily. I never did! I suppose the day will come when a spirit of weariness will take over, but so far it hasn't happened.

Recently, when we were driving on a long trip, my wife kept telling me how tired I must be. She was wrong! I was relaxed and enjoying the ride. At the end of the day when we finally stopped, she said sympathetically, "I know you are tired!" She really was telling me that *she* was tired.

As we drove, she kept saying that she didn't want me to fall asleep. I replied by saying that for me sleep was something that I do—not something that just happens.

I did a lot of thinking about that whole idea. The more I thought, the more I realized that my life is divided into things that I do and things that happen.

I go to sleep when I'm ready. It doesn't happen to me. A sore throat is something that happens. I don't bring it on purposely. Likewise a sneeze happens. I don't willfully do it.

What bothers me are the things that happen in my life that shouldn't be there. For example, when I say something I later regret—something that just pops out—I regret it. The same thing can be said for habits I wish I didn't have.

Most good things are like this. These are some things we do; they don't just happen. We have to work on them.

I didn't fall asleep while driving, but all too often I slumber over the things that really matter. Poor habits make these happen. I'm going to try to do better. Will you join me?

Staples and Hotels

So what's the big deal about stapled hotel tickets? If you do much traveling, you know that when it finally comes to check-out time in a hotel or motel, the clerk either staples the credit card receipt to the hotel bill or doesn't. But the question is usually asked, "Do you want them stapled together?"

It has become such a noticeable routine that I always find myself glancing around the counter as the clerk figures the bill. I'm looking for the stapler, and I'm wondering if this particular hotel has a firm policy of staple or no staple. After enough experience at this, you usually can guess what it will be just by the clerk's personality.

I've found that if the line at the check-out is long, or if it's a large fancy hotel in a big city, you will get your bill stapled whether you like it or not. If you are in a motel in a rural area along the interstate, you are usually asked which you prefer. And if you leave the place early in the morning, the night clerk will sometimes hand you the stapler to do the job yourself.

What has all this got to do with anything? The question is a good one, but the answer is not worth this space. Unless—unless that is, you wonder about the origin of the stapling habit itself. I doubt if the credit card people originally issued a request for all hotels everywhere to staple their receipts to the bill. And I doubt if a large hotel chain issued such a dictum. Considering the number of staples, it could have originated from the stapler companies. But I really think that it came by word of mouth. Some considerate clerk first did it as a courtesy and then it just spread.

Just like most good things. They just spread. Good things are catching. You and I spread happiness.

Think about it next time you get your hotel bill. Then remember how important it is to pass the courtesies of life along as you travel.

Tombstones in the City

In most modern cities, we will find that not all of the highrise buildings are located in the downtown area. I was standing in a friend's office as he talked on the phone, and I was appreciating his view of the city from a couple of miles away. It was a different perspective from that direction.

Just as he hung up the phone, I spotted a cemetery right next to his building. He saw me looking and said, "I tell my pastor that I'm closer to more bodies than he ever has in church."

Business matters soon changed the subject, but I couldn't get that cemetery out of my mind. I not only wondered about the folks buried there, but I also tried to imagine how peaceful that neighborhood must have been before the highrise arrived. Perhaps there was a church where the building now stands. I'm certain that no one of the long-time deceased had ever pictured the city as we now know it.

As I stood up to leave, I looked down at the cemetery again and then thought of the old question we asked as kids years ago. "Do you know why there are fences around graveyards?" I asked. "Why?" my friend replied. I paused and said, "Because people are just dying to get in."

Walking out of the building, I couldn't believe my eyes. The street number marker in front of the building was a tombstone. That's right—a large granite tombstone pronounces both street and number.

Perhaps the building tenants will never notice the cemetery or the tombstone as I did. But now I know what my friend means when he says, "Business is dead." I think I'd move.

Taken as a Compliment

A long-time friend of mine was recently disturbed at a decision I made, and lashed back at me with these words: "You always have been a little offbeat."

I've been told that same thing on other occasions. And I've never taken it as an insult, but only as a compliment. Usually it is said in some form because someone can't agree with some stand I've taken on some matter.

Wouldn't it be dull if we never disagreed with anyone? We would always have to be the same—robot automatons—zombies.

As a "fun exercise," think of which model we would want to use if we could all be the same. Would we all be of one color or one political view or one religious persuasion, or wouldn't it be terrible if we were all of the same sex? Of course the thought is folly, and yet we are all guilty of thinking "He just doesn't think correctly" when we find ourselves in disagreement with someone. Instead of wasting our time and wondering what pattern we all should follow, we should be spending our time in learning to disagree agreeably.

When my friend suggested that I was "offbeat," I thought again of Thoreau's drummer who, the thought implied, was beating a different cadence. And I also thought of my mother who constantly advised me to "be different." "Don't tell me what your friends are thinking! What are you thinking?" she would ask.

So what's wrong with being "offbeat" as long as citizenship and responsibility are exercised with great care. I really appreciated that compliment, even if it wasn't offered as one!

Staying Young

A close friend of mine recently turned eighty. I called to wish him "Happy Birthday," and I asked, "What's it like being eighty?" He replied thoughtfully, "Well, it's a bit like being fifty—only it's more like being seventy-nine."

I laughed aloud because in that humorous response to my question he had said a lot about his approach to life. He later told me that the old bones often felt seventy-nine, but the mind was fifty. And having had the privilege of knowing him for over twenty-five years, I can vouch for the fact that he hasn't changed a bit. He still has the same keen interest in everyone and everything around him. His mind is as sharp as ever. He is filled with new ideas, sound advice, and fresh jokes. He is a pleasure to be around.

About twenty years ago, this same man was commenting on what I thought was a new idea. He somberly looked at me and said, "So you think that's new, eh? Well, son, there just aren't any new ideas." I now know that he didn't mean that. He was only needling a younger colleague, and I find myself making similar statements now and then. But if he really believed that, I am certain he would be an old, old man by now and not a "young eighty."

"What are your secrets to staying so young?" I asked him. His answer was so different. "One thing you do," he said, "is to keep looking for new ideas until the day you die." For him being eighty is more like being fifty, or at least that's the way I see him.

"A Nice Day"

"Have a nice day." How many times a day do we hear that? Everywhere you go now the "have a nice day" wish is given to you whenever you pay a bill or when you talk to someone you don't know.

If you think about it, you will realize that you seldom exchange such words with those you do know. An exception might be as two spouses part for work in the morning, but you would hardly hear it from your lawyer or your doctor as you hang up the phone.

But stop at the dry cleaners or the restaurant and you just can't get away without the maitre d' or the counter clerk saying, "Have a nice day."

I'm never sure what I should say in return. Usually I am thinking of something else anyway, and I'm soundly startled by the good wishes. So when I do say something, it usually comes out in delayed response, such as, "What's that—oh, you too!" If I'm ready and say, "You have a nice day too," it sounds ridiculously redundant. And on those few occasions when I have decided to beat them to the punch, I usually upset their day by saying it first and confusing them, which negates any good wishes I might have had.

I'd rather go back to the good old days when the clerk simply said, "Thanks and y'all come back." And I liked it too when they just counted out your change or hung up the phone with a simple grunt.

But that's not a very friendly attitude, is it? So I'm seriously considering saying to everyone, "Y'all have a nice day, ya heah?"

I Like This Life

It's really very difficult to picture what life will be like after we are gone. I am not referring to what eternal life is like. Folks have speculated on that for years. I'm referring to this life, here on earth, when we're gone.

The first question is, "Will the dog miss me?" But there are better questions than that. What will they say about me? A friend who recently passed away had written his own obituary years ago. All his survivors did was to fill in the details. But what will the mourners say about me, if indeed there are any?

I suppose that what is really important is what I leave for them to say about me. If I am an incorrigible, I can't blame them if they whisper uncomplimentary thoughts. But if I leave some happiness wherever I go, perhaps they will say good things.

It was said of one lady that she brightened every room she entered. What a great thought!

Whatever we think about our own demise, it is probably a good exercise to write about what the occasion might mean to us. My dad tried that once, and when I opened his letter I found these words:

"I think death can be a blessing, especially if it comes

when suffering is becoming too great to endure, as I'm sure it does sometimes. I should be thinking about death more than you should. You are too young, and you have a lot more to accomplish before leaving this life . . . . finishing things you have started and starting new ones. At my age I think more about it than I ever did before, but it doesn't look as bad as it might if I did not have my Christian beliefs.

"I see nothing to change me in adhering to my original beliefs that there is another life which can be a happy one as the Bible says. . . . Of course, I don't understand it all, but I have been led to believe it. I don't understand lots of things that are around me all the time: the seasons, the stars, the moon, childbirth, plants and flowers returning, the individual characteristics of people, the computer, and thousands of other things. I have faith and believe in them as I have in the Bible and its contents. It all helps to make death look a little better. I even hope to see lost loved ones somehow, somewhere. . . . I like this life and so far always have, and even now I'm in the midst of things I'd like to finish, if I can; but the end must come and I realize I can't last this way much longer."

. . . From a letter from my father, a year
before he died at age 84

Furry Rats, I Think!

A very good teenaged friend of mine has some hamsters. She tells me they are hamsters anyway. They look like furry rats to me. And the young lady really loves those hamsters. Though they keep her awake at night doing their endless whirling walking exercise on a track which leads no place, she is fascinated by her little creatures.

Have you ever smelled a hamster? Or has one ever caught your fingers in his pointed teeth? I can't imagine why anyone would want a hamster for a pet. And gerbils are worse. They look more like rats because they have long tails.

Well, in spite of odor, sharp teeth, and rat-like appearance, my friend thinks that her very best friends are those hamsters. Her favorite is a little guy named "Nugget." The other day, when I was trying to show genuine interest in her pets, I took a good look and noticed how much Nugget resembled one of my school teachers from the past. She was the one who taught me the little ditty,

> We have the nicest garbage man;
> He empties our garbage can.
> Mother doesn't like his smell;
> But then, she doesn't know him well.

When I told my young friend about that, she said, "That's why you don't appreciate my hamsters. You don't know them very well."

"What a philosopher she is," I thought. That is why I don't like a lot of people. I don't know them very well. Come to think of it, that's the basis of most of our prejudices. We don't know "those folks" very well.

I walked away from the cage of hamsters with a new appreciation of my role as a human being. I'm going to try to get to know some of the people I don't understand. Maybe I can even learn to like them.

Good old Nugget! I learned from him and now that I know him better, I see that he really is a "jewel" . . . even though he reminds me of my old teacher.

Huh! What! Who!

A businessman stood in my office and suggested that I send a certain document to his place of business. I asked for the address. He paused, took on a blank expression, and then picked up my phone to call his secretary. Without embarrassment he asked her for his own address.

Assuming that he had just moved and had not yet memorized the address, I asked, "Are you in a new office?" He replied, "Oh no, we've been there for years." I couldn't believe it. Here I was doing business with a man who didn't even know where he worked. He knew how to get there, but he didn't know where it was.

At first I wondered about his astuteness. Then I realized that I could take you lots of places in the country without knowing the address. I could go to many airports, then drive right to the hotel or business place, and still not know the mailing address. I would like to assume that it is because busy people only think of the essentials and not the unimportant details, but that's a poor excuse. The truth is that sometimes we simply don't know where we are.

Now I'll admit that I still wonder about the feasibility of doing business with a man who doesn't know where his office is, but I also worry about myself when I'm lost. And most of the time when I'm lost on any subject, it's because I have not paid attention to the seemingly insignificant things in life . . . like street addresses, roses, little dogs, crying children, and aching hearts. I guess I'll keep doing business with my friend, but I wish he would find out what's really important. Someday he may need to find his office, and it will be his secretary's day off. Then he might call me, and I won't know what to tell him.

Deep River and Deep People

We were flying over Arizona on the way to a speaking engagement in Oregon, and my wife was appreciating the clear day and the marvelous view. She was particularly impressed by the deep gorges which narrowly snake their way to the most distant horizon, and which carefully hold deep waters securely in their banks. Even though I knew it wouldn't impress her, I wanted to sound philosophical, so I said, "Some people are like that. They run very deep!"

She slid her glasses down on her nose, grinned a bit, and then said, "Now what does that mean?" I was trapped, so I had to continue.

"Well, some folks are deeper than others," I replied.

"Yes, go on," she replied. I detected that she was more amused than interested in my observations, but I continued anyway.

"Well, I know some people who are only as deep as my shoe." I had heard that one before, but she never had, so she smiled. "And I know some others who are so narrow they could sleep on a clothesline." I had heard that one too but she remained unimpressed.

I went on! "So many folks quit studying and learning and growing as they grow older," I told her. "I like people who have some depth to them, who are willing to examine change without being stuck with yesteryear's traditions."

For the next few minutes, I offered a bit of a homily about the using of one's talents, of setting goals and then achieving them, and of trying to excel at something worthwhile as long as there is life in the body. My mind raced at the thought of things I wanted to learn and to accomplish before it was too late.

I noticed that she wasn't listening. She was in the

process of learning more about beautiful rivers, mountain ranges, and deep rivers. And could there be a more enriching learning experience?

Oh, to Be Young Again!

The man across the counter glanced over his glasses at the young couple in the store, and then he turned to me and said, "Wouldn't it be great to be that age again?" Frankly, I hadn't thought much about it, so I smiled and grunted, but as I drove away I contemplated his question.

The couple was approaching twenty I would guess, although I'm not much of a judge of age. But assuming that I was correct, I began to think of what being nineteen again might mean.

In the first place I would still have to face college and graduate school with all of those tests. I'm not only referring to the entrance exams, but also to midterm exams, final exams, the papers, and all the accompanying footnotes and bibliographies. I really don't want to have to do that again.

Then there would be career choices. Can you imagine what it would be like to select and to train for a career in this world? The choices are more numerous than they used to be it seems, or at least there are a lot of fields today that I didn't hear about then. And most of them involve computers. I never even learned to type correctly. And here's one for you grandfathers. Can you imagine having to start all over again, in this day and time, in raising a family? Some of my grandchildren came over the other day. Am I glad I don't have to do it again! No

P.T.A., no school picnics, no croup in the middle of the night. That nineteen-year-old couple had a lot of things to face that I'm pleased to have behind me.

Would I have chosen another career? I doubt it. Unless I could have gotten on at the state highway department driving one of those grass cutting tractors. That looks like fun!

Shut the Hell Up

A cartoon in a national magazine reminded me of one of the most annoying problems we all face. The scene was the public library. Over the desk the usual sign reading "Silence" was replaced with the sign "Shut the hell up." One man turned to the other and observed, "Everybody's so touchy these days."

That's correct! Sometimes we all fall into the category of "touchy" folks, but we can't take all the blame. Hardly a day goes by when we don't read of someone being shot by another motorist on the freeway, only because the victim blew his horn. And we sense it on the other end of the phone as we conduct our daily business. Try calling a public servant and asking a question about service, or try to expedite a matter, and you are bound to find some folks wearing their feelings on their sleeves. Try to be pleasant and joke a bit, and the reaction often is one you don't expect. Sometimes it seems to be no longer true that a "soft answer turneth away wrath." Sometimes it seems to incur wrath.

So what can be done about it? Here are a few thoughts from a game I play with those I meet. They don't know I'm playing it, and I confess that I don't play it every day, but when I do it puts a bit of interest into the experience of living. It involves keeping score. You have to keep track of every human encounter you have in a single day—every phone call, every personal contact. And you have to rate everyone by "pleasant" or "unpleasant." Every pleasant experience counts two points. Every unpleasant experience removes one point. But after careful and honest examination, if you find that you are the cause of the unpleasant experience, you must lose two points.

Depending on how many people you meet in one day, you can have a fifty or a hundred day, or you can have a minus ten day. When I have that kind of a score, I'm well advised to go off and be by myself.

Try it sometime! "Everybody's touchy" is not quite true, but when I am, I need to correct it.

So Teach Us to Number Our Days

I don't know about your place of business, but mine is full of clock-watchers. Sometimes I even catch myself looking at the time just to see how an unusually dull day might be progressing.

Clock-watchers have a variety of techniques. Some glance at their watches while straightening their shirt sleeves. Others, with exceptional vision, can glance across the conference table to check another person's watch. I even know some who are so bold as to have a small alarm go off as a meeting progresses.

I knew a man years ago who was so bothered by the propensity of clock-watching in our society that he wouldn't even own a watch. When he simply had to know the exact time, he asked someone else. He claimed that he made a lot of new friends that way. I never knew him to be late for anything.

Knowing the time is important if you are meeting many deadlines. But sometimes clock-watching can work against you. I remember a night when they put me in the intensive care unit of a hospital. I wasn't sick enough to be there, but I was told that they were "watching me." All I was watching was the clock. On the plain wall in front of me was a huge clock. When I asked about it, they told me that they needed to see it clearly in case of emergency. I could see it clearly enough, and that was all I could do. They wouldn't let me write, read, or talk on the phone. All I had was that clock, and it reminded me that that segment of my life was wasted. I didn't sleep much that night. I watched that clock.

So if you ever see me glance at my watch, it's because I'm still trying to get that day back. Days are very hard to recover.

Everyone Dies Someplace!

Every once in a while someone publishes a book about medical services abroad. Sometimes the information is in pamphlet form and advises you on simple things such as vaccinations and which foods to avoid. But the last book I read about dealt with serious stuff, like what happens when you have a heart attack in Turkey or an appendicitis attack in India.

Anyone who has traveled overseas has thought about what might happen if they got sick. Can you imagine trying to explain your pain in the chest to a doctor in Siberia, if indeed you could find one? Or how do you say "indigestion" in Dutch? I tried to explain my wife's sick stomach to a pharmacist in Paris, and I was able to get it across only by holding my stomach and gagging. She sold me some medicine and I couldn't understand the directions, but one swallow and the stomach was well.

One thing they never seem to write in these books is that we mustn't forget the fact that the human body is the same anywhere in the world. Facilities, equipment, and medical training differ greatly, but a heart attack is a heart attack wherever you are. And a sore throat hurts the same anyplace. Go ahead and get sick! You'll manage!

I close by reciting a little truth I haven't thought about in years. "Cheer up. You have two chances—one of getting the germ and one of not. And if you get the germ, you have two chances—one of getting the disease and one of not. And if you get the disease, you have two chances—one of dying and one of not. And if you die—well—you still have two chances."

Enjoy your trip and cheer up. Everybody has to die someplace!

Fulfillment

It was late at night, and I was watching television out of the corner of one eye as I read a book with the other. When the announcer told me that I could have a world globe if I subscribed to a respected weekly news magazine, I put the book down and, even though it was late, I dialed the 800 number. I am not one to yield to such TV temptations, but the globe "might make a nice gift," I thought.

The magazine began to come. Then the invoice arrived promising me the "alarm clock" when I returned my check. Whoops! Who said anything about a clock? I wanted a globe!

A letter to the circulation department led nowhere. The proverbial "principle of the thing" forced me to write to the publisher. The answer came that they were turning my letter over to someone else. Then a letter arrived telling me that the globe wasn't advertised on Houston television. Wow! That really got me! A picture of a globe had come over my TV—in my den—in Houston, Texas.

By now many of you are saying, "Forget it, Bill. You can't win." Well—you are wrong! I have a letter to prove it. I am going to get my globe.

Now the point of all of this is that I ran into a new title. The man who finally solved the problem is Vice President for Fulfillment. Isn't that great? I am not sure what his duties are (surely he doesn't ship globes around the country), but I do like the title. When I get my promotional gift, I will be fulfilled. Can you imagine the responsibility that title carries with it? His wife and kids expect him to be able to "fulfill." His religious leader expects more out of him. And maybe, just maybe, his fellow vice presidents stop into his office in the midst of their burnout experiences so that he can give them the inspiration for their own fulfillment.

Personally, I like the title. And I like the role he filled. I know that somewhere on my new globe there will be a blank spot. I will label it "A Man of Fulfillment." The world is bound to be better. And if I ever get a chance to meet him, I might even be tempted to kiss his ring. After all, he's going to bring me the world—or at least the globe.

Well, What Do You Know?

Back in 1927 in an industrial plant, an experiment was being conducted which would change the world. Until then no one had thought much about motivation in the work environment.

In attempting to see what might happen, management increased lighting in the work area and production went up. Then they tried it the opposite way by dimming the bright lights, and production went up again.

A conclusion was reached that had nothing to do with lighting. They had stumbled onto the simple fact that if you pay attention to the employees, production goes up.

The truth they discovered in that industrial setting was not new. Even the ancients recorded the idea that when you care for a person there usually is a positive response.

The positive-support concept is not just for industry. It works everywhere. Smile at the butcher, and you will get better service. Be nice to the traffic cop, and even receiving a ticket won't be as bad as it will be if you give him a hard time.

And all of us know that it works in the family too. Show a genuine interest in a spouse or a son or a daughter, and the positive reactions begin to flow.

Often our industrial genius is simply a practical application of an ancient truth.

Arrival

There are all sorts of ways to know when you have really "arrived". There are the usual indications, such as title, business success, and financial achievements, but there are other hints as well.

For example, when your children grow old enough to seek your advice, you have "arrived." You also have made it when you have lived in the same house long enough to make the last mortgage payment. But there are other signs too.

Recently we were enjoying dinner in a nice restaurant with a younger couple. The younger woman ordered decaffeinated coffee. The rest of us ordered regular coffee. When the waiter arrived, guess who got the Sanka? The same waiter also assumed that the bill was mine too. I accepted both as a token of "arrival."

Perhaps you have noticed other symbols. People your own age begin to call you "sir" or "ma'am." Policemen will look younger, and schoolteachers no longer will seem to be eighty-five. And if you really are in the age of arrival, your secretary will be younger than your daughter.

At first all this is a shock, but all that it actually means is that you have finally "arrived."

I'll bet you younger folks can't wait!

A Pause for Respect

Since the beginning of recorded history, we can find references to humankind's ceremonies for burial of the dead. Customs vary throughout the world, but they also vary widely throughout different parts of the United States.

Recently I attended a funeral service in Alabama. Being in Alabama was in itself a reason to think that I might find customs which were new to me, and being in a rural area guaranteed it. Actually I didn't find many differences, but I did find a custom which passed from the local scene several years ago.

Can you remember when the traffic stopped as a funeral procession passed by? It wasn't too many years ago when you could see it happening right on the streets of the city, but you don't see it anymore. Perhaps the freeways have spoiled our manners, but admittedly the traffic jam would be dangerous if we pulled over each time a line of "lights-on" cars passed.

As I rode the miles from the funeral home to the red-dirt Alabama graveside, I was impressed at how everyone pulled off the side of the highway. Large trucks did it, and so did the fancy sports cars driven by young people.

At first I thought how out-of-date the people were—how behind the times. And then I realized that some customs are worth keeping. For a moment those who paused got a chance to remember their own mortality as they honored the dead. What an opportunity!

An "Act of God"?

Recently lightning hit the cathedral at York, England. According to reports, "the force of the blast splintered the cathedral's thirteenth-century oak beams and sent the roof of the south transept collapsing in flames to the flagstone below." I remember seeing that cathedral, and while there is "sameness" to the experience of cathedral touring, there remains a fixed picture of Yorkminster in my mind.

It was then reported that a debate was going on in England, and especially in church circles, as to whether that particular storm was more than just an average "act of God."

It seems that some of the folks don't like the views of the newly consecrated bishop, and they have assumed that God didn't either, and therefore the devastating lightning occurred.

Now I wouldn't think of using this space to take a position on a theological issue as heated as "divine retribution." You will have to join whatever segment of the debate that strikes your fancy, if indeed you wish to enter at all. I have simply brought up the illustration to comment on this whole "act of God" idea.

We see the phrase "act of God" in insurance policies, legal documents, and in all sorts of contracts. Poor God gets blamed for everything! It seems that if you really wanted to make a fortune, you could start a nonprofit organization to "put the blame somewhere else," or to "remove God from the contracts." You could charge a dollar for membership and get rich very quickly. Lots of folks stand ready to remove God from everything else, so why not the fine print of insurance policies? It just doesn't seem fair!

No Power!

Some people experience earthquakes, some typhoons, and some have ice storms! Where I live, we have hurricanes. What a storm! All of the warnings from the weather service did not prepare us for the fury of those winds. When Mother Nature decides to prune her trees, she really gets it over with in a hurry. Now if we could only find a practical way to get all of that firewood to the folks in the colder climates.

I was one of the fortunate ones to be without power for several days. While everyone around me was griping about power loss, I was rejoicing. Oh, I admit I felt sorry for the folks who were suffering from it, and I hated to lose the food in the freezer, but the loss of power was basically a good experience.

With no power I did not have to watch television. Of course, no one makes me do it anyway, but with the thing sitting there I frequently turn it on when I should be doing something more constructive. A lack of air conditioning and other comforts to which we have become acquainted, all became a reminder of how fortunate we are to live in these times. While I would hate to return to "no power" days forever, it really wasn't all that bad. It wouldn't take long to get used to living that way.

Listening to the talk shows on my battery-operated radio, I got the distinct impression that not everyone shared my views. I couldn't believe the complaints being made against the power company. When you inconvenience people who are used to creature comforts, they really can fuss and gripe.

That second night, with no lights to read by, and with no other electrical distractions, I found myself sitting on the porch in total darkness. No AC units were droning in the distance. No street light was in my eyes. All I could hear were tree frogs and buzzing mosquitoes. Usually we have to go miles away to get that solitude and here it was—right in our own backyard. I don't need another hurricane to remind me, but I surely appreciated the reminders from this one. I wonder what else is in my yard!

"Where There's a Will . . ."

Planning a will is an exercise we all must engage in, and, depending on our general outlook on life, the experience can be pleasant or terrifying. But pleasant or not, it's necessary.

When my attorney and I sat down to update my will, I was reminded of the passing years. The first time I made a will I was interested in what would happen to my three small children. Now they have children of their own. How time flies!

In my work I have the opportunity to visit with people concerning their final distribution. It's interesting how some people react to the subject. I know some who don't want to discuss it because they don't seem to believe that it will happen. But it will happen, and if you have been putting it off, today is not too soon to do the job.

I also get the opportunity to read some wills after they have been probated. Most of the ones I've seen are patterned after the way the person has lived. A person who is generous in life probably will be generous in the estate distribution. A person who has been tight, stingy, and self-centered often will exhibit these characteristics in preparing the will. And that's understandable. Since a will is supposed to be prepared when a person is in "sound mind," sound mind characteristics do come through.

What we say in our will is sometimes the only "voice" we will have in the future. Do you want immortality? Better update your will! You might see it as a reminder of mortality but it's also a symbol of stewardship.

Working on My Day Off

An editorial in a national newspaper recently called for a National Work Day, not another day off from work.

My first thought was that I was already working hard enough on my job, and even if we had a National Work Day, I couldn't do more. Then I admitted to myself that this simply wasn't so. Obviously I had not reached 100 percent of output. Does anyone?

Then my thoughts shifted from myself and my own work habits to those who work for me and their habits. It is amazing how much they do accomplish, but I can't think of one who is giving all he/she has for the cause.

There are those who work long hours. I am sometimes guilty of that myself, but most of the time I have to do it because I didn't arrange the rest of my time in proper order. Then I notice folks around me doing the same thing. I wonder if all of those phone calls are really business related. And I wonder if they get back on time from breaks and lunch periods.

Well, if we don't put out 100 percent, what is the percent figure? Are your workers giving your company as much as 75 percent of their potential? I hope so.

I'll continue to keep an eye on them, but I'll also examine my own percentage figure. Like—What is my real work output potential? Or—How much am I really getting out of life, or putting in for that matter? Then there is that ever-motivating question—I wonder what percent of my total life I already have lived?

Maybe we should call it Working and Living Day. Or it could be known as "Watch Me Go for It" day. What would life be like without work?

A Monkey on the Freeway

As I was about to leave the office, I noticed a huge, stuffed monkey near the back door. He was bright purple in color and had a full set of white whiskers. On impulse I decided to borrow him overnight.

I put the monkey (I guess he should be called a gorilla) on the front seat and fastened him securely with the seat belt. He sat up a bit taller than I did, and as we went down the freeway in the rush hour traffic, we received some interesting reactions.

A carload of little children frantically waved at my stuffed companion. I had expected something like that. But then two painters came by with their faces almost as painted as the monkey's, and when they saw him they slowed down and gave me a thumbs-up signal. At the red light, a guy in the pickup next to me yelled, "Right on, pardner."

The police car that passed hesitantly caused me the most enjoyment. The young cop did a double-take, slowed down, and then shook his head. But I detected a grin which he didn't want me to see. I'm sure he wondered if I was breaking any laws.

Almost everyone slowed down. No, I didn't cause any accidents! People actually loosened up a bit, and while they didn't really pause to smell the roses, they did relax enough to get a glimpse at the purple ape with white whiskers.

The mass-transit folks have been trying to solve our freeway problems for years. I now know how to do it. All we have to do is to issue purple monkeys for every car, and the result will be less tension on the road. I have a purple monkey if you want to borrow it.

I'm Glad to Be Running At All

A friend offered to pick me up at the office and take me to lunch. I welcomed the opportunity, and so a date and time were set. Fortunately my window faces the parking lot so I was able to keep other chores going as I watched for him. As the time approached, I stood up to reach for my coat. I'm a stickler for being on time.

Just at the moment he was due to arrive, the phone rang, and he announced he was "running late."

I wondered where that phrase came from originally. I'm going to look it up someday, but my imagination ran away with me as I waited. Did it come from the days when messages were carried by messengers who ran from one place to another? I can imagine that on rainy, muddy days they would "run late." They surely had days when they just didn't feel well and "ran late."

Or could it be that the phrase came out of the railroad era when all railroaders consulted their watches with regularity just to be certain that the engine would "run well" so that they didn't "run late"?

Maybe my friend was being totally candid when he said he was running late. It is possible that he was jogging late into the night and just couldn't get up on time.

Well, whatever the reason, he was late and he messed up my day's schedule. By the way, he finally arrived, apologized for "running late," and then proceeded to keep us "running late" into the afternoon. I'm not sure where we got the phrase, but we all know what it means. I'm going to try to be on time except for my own funeral for which I hope to keep everyone waiting for a long, long time!

We All Scream for Ice Cream

My grandchildren, like most other children, like ice cream. Recently we all went to get an ice cream cone, and while I watched their enjoyment, my mind through memory returned me to my own childhood. How times have changed! And how did those lines go? "I scream, you scream, we all scream for ice cream."

Ice cream cones cost a nickel then. I'm sure of that because I remember dropping mine on the pavement once, and my dad told me that there were no more nickels. So my mother and I shared hers. In Mr. Davis' Ice Cream Store, located not far from our home, there were only a few flavors. I can remember when chocolate fudge ripple came along and how good that tasted for a change. Now going to an ice-cream store involves a choice of a host of flavors, and some of the names are enough to discourage even an ice-cream lover.

If you are old enough perhaps you can recall the homemade ice cream that used to turn up on special occasions. No, I don't mean the kind we make in these modern electric homemade gadgets. I'm thinking of the kind you turn by hand. There was something special about that taste, and since there was no freezer to pop it in until tomorrow, it all had to be eaten before you went to bed. What memories! I do like ice cream!

One thing brought me back to reality. Kids still don't know how to eat ice cream without spilling it. Good grief, it's dripping all over the place. Next time I'll take the ice cream to them instead of taking them to the ice cream!

What Are You Advertising?

Can you remember the man who carried the sandwich board signs during the Depression? For the benefit of the young, these were two pieces of wood or heavy cardboard carried on the front and the back of the bearer, who was literally "sandwiched" in between. They often advertised Joe's Beanery or some such place. They weren't paid much, but it was an honest living.

Now there is a new way to advertise, and it's not television or even the blimp. If you can get someone to wear your jeans or your T-shirt, you can spread the word quickly and, what's more, he will pay for the privilege.

I have a teenage friend who advertises and doesn't even realize it. He wears a Bechtel hat (even in restaurants when he's eating), an Addidas shirt, Levi jeans, and Nike shoes. All of the labels are openly displayed. The funny thing is that he is anti-establishment in his philosophy, and yet he has fallen for the best of the tricks of Madison Avenue and doesn't even know it. He serves as a continuous billboard.

Now before you laugh at him, go out and check your car. You probably have a sticker or plastic plate on the back which gives the name of your car dealer. And if, like me, you make the dealer remove it as a condition of sale, you still carry the name of the car in letters or design. And that brings to mind a "Z" car owned by the snail who changed the "Z" to "S" so that his friends could say, "Look at that escargot."

Now if I could only get folks to advertise for me! There must be a way.

No Room for Guilt

A good friend of mine recently had a terrible guilt trip. He was forced to sign a paper that wasn't quite legal. It was all done so quickly that he didn't think much about it, but when the document had been sent off, the feelings set in. How guilty, how terrible he felt.

I listened to the whole story. It was wrong to do the deed, but it really didn't hurt anybody. And yet how my friend suffered. Nothing I could say seemed to help. I assured and reassured, but the guilt wouldn't leave. The more guilty he felt, the better I liked my friend.

Where does guilt come from in the first place? Guilt comes from within as the forces of good within us struggle with the forces of evil—especially if we have taken part in some evil. It stands to reason that if we don't have much good in us, we won't feel much guilt. So the longer he was guilty, the better I liked him because I knew that there was a lot of good in him.

This is an oversimplification of a complex and potentially dangerous problem, but those who aren't sensitive and caring people don't feel a lot of guilt. Or at least they don't recognize it.

My friend kept saying, "I feel so guilty." I kept saying, "I like you because you do." And it's true! I can always like the person who does wrong and knows it much more than I can appreciate the person who does wrong and never realizes it.

Should we then do wrong to be liked? Of course not, but when we do we can remember that someone likes us anyway, and that we can't worry about what has already happened. Tomorrow is another day! And another day always means another chance. Hooray for tomorrow.

Write!

Recently I received a letter from a friend who lives several states away. Unlike some of the mail today, this letter was on time, but its condition could hardly be a credit to the Postal Service. It was torn, dirty, and terribly wrinkled, and it had something that resembled grease on the back.

My friend never would have sent me that kind of a letter. He is a meticulously neat man who always dresses well, writes well, and speaks well. In fact, he would been embarrassed if he had seen the condition of his letter.

Fortunately only the envelope was destroyed, but it started me to wondering what the mail might have looked like back in the days of the Pony Express. Obviously my letter must have been caught in some modern post office sorting machine, and I guess I should be glad that I received it in any condition. But what about the letter that had to get through even in the "snow, sleet, rain, or hail" in the old days? My imagination tells me that those letters were worn and dirty too. Some must have had bullet holes in them from wild gun-shots from some outlaw along the way. Some might have had arrows piercing the message.

Then I began to wonder about the mode of travel for the mail since the horserider took it from place to place. Now it goes by truck, train, and plane, and the increased population must have increased the problems. Actually, it's quite a miracle that it ever gets delivered as fast as it does when you think about it.

Back to my torn letter! My neat and clean friend was only sending his greetings and best wishes. I can accept that sort of letter regardless of the condition. Can't you?

Born Too Soon?

I was born too soon! Or at least I was born "not so bright." I'll leave that determination to the reader, but I have a confession to make and I don't care who reads it. I'm having a hard time adjusting to the computer age.

I've tried to adapt! When everyone convinced me that the accounting office simply had to have a computer to be efficient, we acquired one and now we have double the staff to operate it. And everytime I need a report in a hurry, I'm told that the computer is "down," and the result is that I am soon "down" too.

Computers have brought a whole new language with them. I'm too old to try to understand bytes, floppy disks, disassemblers, and the dot-matrix system. I want to chuckle when I hear about being "on line," or when someone refers to the joystick with analog-to-digital inputs along with four TTL outputs. I remember one computer salesman who promised with a straight face that I would have automatically scaled and numbered pie charts from numerical data, along with exponential, parabolic, and sinusoidal plots.

Now I want to assure you that I respect computer people and that I realize I live in the computer age. Please don't call me to tell me that we couldn't have made it to the moon without the computer. I know all that. I just don't understand it. I was born too soon.

I also realize that I'm probably the only one who is "in the dark," but I feel better now that I've confessed it. It's really great to be in the company of all who do understand these things! Cheer up and don't be too discouraged with me. I've decided to take a course to keep up with the rest of you.

No Mail?

Even in this day of high postage costs I seem to be on everyone's list. I really don't mind. The catalogs I didn't ask for are fun to examine. The requests for money for all sorts of good causes don't bother me either. (I've even been known to write a few of those myself.) I don't even get upset when some high-pressure salesman follows his letter with a phone call. I enjoy studying his style.

But the letters which do bother me are from the "religious" groups which promise me all sorts of miracles in my life if I send in a few dollars. They bother me because I know that many folks out there fall for that approach, while the sender is the one who really reaps the benefits of their naïveté.

Last week I got a letter from a "minister" in Washington, D.C., who claimed to have one of the biggest churches in the District of Columbia. He wrote to me, a form letter of course, as "Dear Chosen One." He promised that I would be blessed with all sorts of money if I sent a contribution to his building fund. He even included a testimony from one respondee who is now driving a Lincoln Continental.

First I was amused. Then I was annoyed as I realized how many would respond. What really got me was that this "church" has only a post office box as a return address.

Bring on the "fun mail." When I don't want to read it, I can always toss it away. But deliver us all from the mail which I know will take advantage of a lot of innocent people who will never be driving Continentals. I'd like to meet that minister, but my car won't go that far.

Afraid of Giants?

A friend of mine shared this thought with me. He suggested that when the Israelites faced the giant Goliath, the onlookers said, "He is too big. We cannot possibly defeat him." The boy David looked at the giant and said, "He's so big I can't miss him."

I went right back to my office and looked at my problems. The illustration stuck with me for a few days, and I began to see all of my challenges in a different light. No longer were they giants which would overwhelm me. They suddenly became huge targets which couldn't be missed. Once more a Bible story made new sense.

The story from the Old Testament ends when David takes his shepherd's sling and skillfully plants a stone right on Goliath's huge forehead, and the giant is killed.

How does your story end? Did the giants in your life get you, or did you get them? As I look back on my own life, I see a few which whipped me. But I also see many which I was able to defeat. There are a few facing me right now. In fact they are so large that I can't possibly walk away from them to a place where I can't see them. They loom over my horizon when I look in any direction. They are always there. But now that I've been reminded of David, I know that because of their size I can't miss them. I'm going to be able to conquer them in time.

I may not run as fast as I used to in my youth, but my solution will be on dead center. Life is too rich to be threatened by giants. So the next time one comes my way, I'm going to reach for the proverbial slingshot and let him have it.

Just One Word, Please!

Do you want to have some fun—and learn something about yourself in the process? If your feelings get hurt easily, I need to warn you that it could be painful. Here's what it's all about.

A couple of weeks ago one of my staff members was upset with one of my decisions, and she said, "I could summarize you in about twenty-five words." Since I wasn't ready to hear that much about myself, I replied, "How about summing me up in one word?" She did! I'll not tell you the word because it's not important in this context, but what she did do was to start me on a quest for the words which sum me up.

I've said to my loved ones and associates, "What single word do you think of when you think of me?" The results have been fascinating. I won't share those either, but I can report that I've had a new look at what others think when they think of me. Sometimes the words have been the ones I hoped I was projecting. Other times the words have not been very complimentary. But always the summing-up words have been revealing.

Try it. Ask someone to sum you up in one word. But brace yourself. You might be surprised.

Tomorrow Is Coming

I was saying good-night to the workers as they left the plant. One young man nodded, walked past, and then wheeled around and blurted out, "I hope tomorrow will be better than today." He was so emphatic that all who heard him chuckled. No one seemed to know of anything which might have caused him a bad day, but the frantic way in which he spoke of tomorrow made us assume that whatever had spoiled his day must have been really bad.

His reply to a simple day's farewell has rung in my ears since that day. Maybe he had had a rough day, but chances are he was merely expressing hope. And who hasn't expressed the same hope for tomorrow? It's not that today was so terrible. It's just a wish that tomorrow will be better.

That's why we work so hard. It's why we invest in retirement funds. It's why we take our medicine on time, and it's why we go to the dentist. Maybe the reason we visit our house of worship is because we have hope that tomorrow will be even better than today.

The optimist is one who looks forward to tomorrow being a better day. The pessimist assumes that tomorrow cannot possibly be better. Indeed, it might even be worse.

A popular cry today is "Give me the good old days." Personally I enjoy their memories, which always make them seem better, but I prefer to count them as just that—memories—and I eagerly look forward to tomorrow. In fact my fervent prayer is that tomorrow will be better than today, as good as it has been.

Look for a better day tomorrow, and I'll bet you will find it. But live in the yesterdays and you'll eventually be miserable.

The Blahs!

A cartoon in *The Wall Street Journal* recently made me chuckle. It pictured the doctor as he completed a routine physical examination, and he was saying to the patient, "Let's be honest. We really don't know a whole lot about the 'blahs.'"

Have you ever had the blahs? Unless you are very special, the answer is "Yes." All of us have experienced a condition which really cannot be defined. The doctor in the cartoon is being very honest because no one really does know very much about the blahs.

Actually there is not much known about the condition because the causes are so varied. Some people get lingering cases of the blahs simply because someone speaks harshly to them. Some get the "disease" because they catch it from others. It isn't true that if you laugh the world will laugh with you, but if you weep you will weep alone. There are plenty of folks who enjoy catching the blahs from you and will be glad to weep right along with you. Whole families and entire office crews can get the blahs at the same time. We are fortunate that the whole world doesn't get them at the same time.

One of the best words that defines my own strain of the blahs is lethargy. Fortunately it doesn't happen very often, but on those occasions when I catch it, I become very lethargic. And one of the reasons it doesn't happen often is because I won't permit it. Knowing that I am susceptible, I try to fill my life with so many alternatives that I just don't have time to get down. Other things can stop me completely, but I refuse to let the blahs take over.

I am convinced that the medicine for this ailment is available without visiting the drugstore. If you happen to be running out, it would be wise to build up a supply. Call it faith, hope, or whatever, but life is too short for the blahs. Besides, they really don't know much about it anyway!

Dear Old Dad Is Me

After my father's death, I suddenly realized that I was the family patriarch. "Good grief," I thought, "I'm too young for that."

Then I faced it honestly and remembered that it was true. Age has been creeping up on me for sometime. There are all kinds of symptoms.

First there is the grandparent role. It seems to me that my grandparents were always a whole lot older than I am, but when I stop to calculate, that simply isn't so. But didn't they seem old?

Then there are the experiences of yesteryear which will date you too. When I told the cameraman at a local TV station that I had made my first television commercial over twenty-five years ago, he looked at me in awe. He was only about twenty-two himself. I must have seemed like Father Time to him.

Then the one that really gets me is when I tell my kids of Mr. Smith. When I was a small boy, I used to visit Mr. Smith, and he rocked in his rocking chair and spilled long cigar ashes all over his vest. He had a shiny gold piece hanging on a chain which draped from pocket to pocket, and he would delight in showing me the "monkey" in the reflection. What is it about the story of Mr. Smith that makes me think of the passing years? Well, he was a Civil War veteran, that's what! I'm old enough to have known a Civil War veteran.

Some of you could look back even further. I really feel sorry for the ones of you who have so much youth that you've had time to accumulate only a few memories. Oh nuts, who am I kidding? I really am the family patriarch. The only consolation is that all of you are adding age at exactly the same rate of speed.

A Glimpse and a Glance

While sitting in a crowd of people in the county courthouse, I looked around and noticed that most of the folks were reading. Some had the morning paper, some had what appeared to be inter-office memos, but most were reading paperback books.

To relieve my boredom I glanced around at the titles near me, expecting to find mysteries or science fiction or cheap love novels, but I was surprised to find that the titles had to do with things of a self-help nature. I was so surprised that I wandered about the room trying to catch a glance at the rest of the titles. And the trend continued as I saw subjects on "Coping," "Improving," "Faith," "Self-Image," and one was even entitled, *How to Be a Better Person*. Not remembering the various bestseller lists containing such titles, I wondered, "Why so many in one room at a time?"

Could it be that folks find themselves in such a complex and changing environment that personal improvement becomes a priority to solve community problems? Perhaps the mental-health experts are correct when they predict that a large portion of the population will be emotionally affected by this "maze" in which we live. And maybe these books are a way out. Or maybe a day in community service brings out the best in people and their reading on that day reflects that good feeling.

Whatever the reason, I was pleased at the findings of my random glance around the room. If we can all take up some self-help or improvement literature, maybe the world will improve. Have you read a book on how to cope lately? I would hate to admit that I was only "looking around" while my fellow jurors were improving themselves!

What Did You Say to the Queen?

There was a terrible shooting in a local store just a few weeks ago. It was a domestic dispute. The husband arrived when the store opened, approached his wife who was a cashier in the store, and unloaded his 38-caliber pistol into her body and the wall. The onlookers were terrified as bullets flew.

On entering the store the man had to pass an armed, uniformed security guard, so after he had shot six times he put his gun on the counter, lifted up his arms, and waited. He fully expected to be apprehended. When no one grabbed him, he walked past the security guard and ran down the street.

It is hard to understand why a security guard who goes through extensive training, and then hires on to protect persons and goods, will stand still and never even say "Halt." It was the biggest opportunity in his life. He could have made the papers, been on TV, received rewards, and gone on for the rest of his life with a big accomplishment under his belt. But he blew it. When it was all over, he went back into obscurity. He had missed his big chance.

The whole thing reminded me once more of the nursery rhyme concerning the pussy cat who went to London to visit the queen, but when asked what she did there, she replied, "I chased a little mouse under a chair." Faced with the opportunity to meet the queen, the cat couldn't resist following her habit of chasing the mouse. The security guard, when faced with his big opportunity to achieve, couldn't resist following his habit of doing nothing. And nothing is just what he did. How tragic!

But the illustration hurts a bit, for I too have let great opportunities pass me by as I have followed old habits. Some of our habits need re-examination.

It's not too late to meet the queen.

Mom Liked Him Best

I got to thinking about my brother the other day. The old boy is seven years older than I, and recently had a heart attack and a bypass, and—well, I've been thinking about my brother!

If you have an older brother, I suspect that some of your thoughts could parallel mine. Remember when you were a kid, how your older brother would involve you in his mischief, and how you went along thinking you were on safe ground because your brother recommended it, only to have him blame it all on you when you got caught? Did you ever think Mother liked him best? It's no wonder!

I'll never forget the day my brother went off to war. I was only eleven and the bottom seemed to drop out of my life. My idol was leaving. Of course I never called him that then, but that's what he was. And every souvenir from the European front became my most prized possession. I even remember his dog tag serial number—33718639. And when the messenger brought those terrible telegrams into the neighborhood from time to time, I gulped and hoped that one wouldn't be about my brother.

Then the war was over, and the biggest day in my life still has to be the day I watched him walk in and unpack his duffle bag and then settle down to treat me like a little brother again. I survived all of that, and as the years went on we became the closest of friends. I've always looked up to him as my older brother. It's a mark of respect . . . and tradition.

But after that bypass, when we had a long chat over the phone, I didn't feel like the little brother anymore. We were just brothers—very close friends. And we both remembered how nice it would be if we could stop long enough in our individual "busyness" just to reminisce. If we ever do, we'll laugh a bit, and maybe we'll even cry some, and if I'm lucky I'll become that little brother again, and he'll be my big brother. And for that moment I'll be able to remind him again that "Mother always liked him the best." No wonder! He is best! Isn't your big brother?

No Motivation Here

A few weeks ago I attended a management seminar which was designed to motivate the participants to do a better job of management. I have been to many such sessions over the years and usually come away inspired and challenged. At least I expect to be reminded of my shortcomings so that I can try to do better. But this time the lecture was so dull that the motivation was all negative. In fact, about one half of the group was motivated to leave after the coffee break.

The leader of the seminar certainly was well qualified. He had degrees from several leading universities and had obviously been successful in operating his own research and training company. He certainly had conducted such groups before. I wondered why he was so dull.

My mind wandered as I listened to his drone. His illustrations were old, and his funny stories weren't even funny, so rather than doze off I wondered what was wrong with him. Maybe he was feeling bad, but his color looked OK, and he moved as if he wasn't hurting. Or perhaps his wife had said something to spoil his day and, therefore, his presentation. Possibly he had received some bad news just as he was coming into the room. Whatever it was, I thought it had to be serious.

I stayed in the room and tried to look interested, but as he went on and on, I wished I had left too. He didn't improve, and as my colleagues grunted occasionally I tried to decide if it was from amazement, agreement, or indigestion. Then it hit me! I was getting a beautiful lesson in reverse motivation, and I realized also that too many times I had been an expert in that field myself. If the lecturer's attitude and approach could work so negatively on me and on the others in the audience, I realized my own attitude could do the same as I interacted with people at work or in other activities.

I am sure that he didn't expect anyone to be motivated in quite the way I was, but his terrible lecture has made me more careful in my own motivational management. I really owe thanks to that dull guy.

You're It!

You're it! Do you remember those games of tag we played when we were kids? Suddenly a burst of energy would hit us during recess on the school grounds, and we would dash up to a friend, hit him gently and say, "You're it!" He was expected to respond by chasing you until he tapped you and said, "Now you're it!" As I look back on it, I realize what a silly game it was. I also wonder if I ever really had enough energy to play that hard. I guess I did!

As we get older there are other variations of the "it" game. A few years ago, a religious group had a campaign featuring the slogan, "I've found it," and bumper stickers announcing that slogan were seen all over the community. It wasn't long before the inevitable response appeared on other bumpers: "I never lost it."

The other day I noticed a bumper sticker on a broken-down pickup truck with yet another variation on the "it" theme. It simply stated, "This is it." At first I wondered what was being proclaimed. I saw nothing on that truck to convince me that the ultimate in luxury driving comfort had been reached. The grizzly looking driver hardly could be proclaiming his own attributes. I still am confused and have no idea what "it" meant in that case.

Then the truth came to me. "It," I surmised, is anything you want "it" to be. In a game of tag "it" means the person who needs to run faster so he won't be "it." In the bumper sticker which perplexed me, I discovered that "this" was "it." My problem in that case is that I'm not sure what "this" is.

At least the driver of the truck didn't misuse the English language by saying, "This is where it's at." But what if he had! I still wouldn't have known what "it" was.

So the question remains for me. What is "it"? And further questions come to mind. Will I recognize "it" when "it" is finally discovered, or is "it" really "this" after all? The final question is the most difficult. Are you "it" or am I?

The Search for the Stress

You hear a lot about stress these days. In fact, we all reach the age when our various advisers tell us to cut down on stress. My doctor looked at me recently and said, "I won't define it for you, but you need to get rid of the stress in your life."

It usually follows that someone will suggest that your vocation causes you stress. Advice will come from all

103

corners about reducing work hours, delegating more, and letting someone else take care of the problem.

You might call it rationalization, but I'm convinced that my job doesn't cause me stress. There are stressful parts of the job to be sure, but most of these simply occurred and didn't belong there anyway. Stress comes from many sources.

Usually the adviser prescribes golf courses, fishing holes, barrooms, and night clubs as good places to unwind. And maybe these forms of recreation are always mentioned because so many people do dislike their vocations and consider these other things as means of escape.

I submit that what causes stress in one person does not cause it in another. Most of you wouldn't want my job and for you it would be stressful, as yours would be for me. But my job is what I do. It's a part of me. And what's more, I like doing it. Having to follow you around the golf course would be stressful for me. And I couldn't think of anything I'd rather not do than to have a "happy hour" stop on my way home.

My dislike of the golf course or the "happy hour" doesn't mean that I don't recreate. I do, and some of my methods would cause stress in you. I doubt if zipping through the traffic on a motorcycle would really appeal to a cane-pole fishing enthusiast.

All of this is to suggest that we really haven't faced the facts about ourselves if we can't find the sources of our stress. Don't always assume that it's your job that does it. A word of caution is in order. Sometimes when we find it, it's not what we expected. Sometimes the truth hurts!

I'm convinced that we would all be healthier if we started the stress search early in our lives.

What's Your Opinion?

There is a lot of difference in the meaning of the words "fact" and "opinion." Have you ever noticed that we get a whole lot more "opinions" than we do "facts"? In this scientific age, where so much can be measured accurately in the test tube, you would think that "fact" would take over, but, alas, "opinion" is what we hear most often.

Politicians and political-action groups are always expressing "opinions." Sometimes they call it "fact," and their opponents never believe them anyway. But we listen and we take sides and we enjoy it all because it's the way we do political business. Most of us are even willing to contribute a dollar of our hard-earned money so that some candidates can express an opinion. We call it "politics."

Religious leaders do it too. We all can go to our different houses of worship and come out with different "opinions." And if you haven't been to yours lately, just tune in on the religious TV or radio folks and see how much hard fact you hear there. In religion we can get away with it too, only we don't call it "opinion." We call it "interpretation."

And in medicine we find it also. There are a lot of facts in that profession, but many times the doctor reaches into his bag of experience and gives an "opinion." Occasionally the physician will call in an "associate" for another "opinion." In medicine they call "opinion giving" a part of the "practice."

If you really want to get far from facts, go deep into anybody's woods and ask for some information about a person of another race or religion. In those areas we can get lots of opinions and few facts (if any). We call that "prejudice," which has also been referred to as "looking down on something you are not up on."

Remember the TV show called "Dragnet" back in the 1950s? Jack Webb never cracked a smile when he would say, "Just give me the facts, ma'am."

That's what we all need. We need the facts. Can you imagine how we would cleanse the world if we all started giving facts. Opinion has its place, but I would appreciate it if my political leaders and my religious leaders and my doctors and my friends would just give me "the facts." Ouch, not too fast now! Sometimes the facts hurt!

Fake or Genuine?

On one of the recent television exposés, an oil painting was featured. Most of the experts claimed that it was a fraud. They outlined all sorts of reasons as to why it could not be genuine. One even said that he was sure the fake artist was laughing at the whole thing. Only those who purchased the painting for the museum claimed it was authentic.

I was fascinated by the things which seemed to be out of place. The costumes of the period, for example, simply were not correct. The fingers and hands weren't relaxed enough. The facial features, especially the eyes, weren't genuine. I don't know much about great paintings, but I was convinced that what we were looking at was a genuine fraud.

The whole story of that painting and its obvious inaccuracies has been in my mind since, and I have been looking at folks around me. Some of the costumes people wear don't seem to belong in this period of time. While we don't see as many folks in outlandish garb as we did in the 1960s, we still see some outfits which seem to come from a distant planet.

I've also looked at the fingers and hands of those around me. I see many which aren't relaxed at all. They have chewed fingernails, nervous twitches, and fingers drumming in boredom. I've even looked at the eyes! Some dance from place to place, and some can't possibly look into mine.

All of this is to say that not all fakes are on the canvas. We are surrounded by them every day. The nervousness and the obvious unrest are symbols of the pressures of our time.

I suppose that it would be wise to ask ourselves how we are doing. Are we fakes or are we genuine? Only time will judge the painting. What will history do with you and with me?

Somebody Listen!

Have you ever had the feeling that you could solve the problem, whatever it is, if you only had the chance? I mean, have you ever had the solution, but no one seemed to want to listen?

I was sitting in traffic on one of our freeways the other day. The traffic was stopped dead, and suddenly I had the answer. With a few signs and an adjustment or two in the off ramps, I knew that that particular bottleneck could be cleared forever. But I didn't know who to tell!

Then I had some ideas about crime too. I was sure that I could solve some of the problems which plague our police department if only I had the chance to try. But, I reasoned, who would listen to me anyway? So I did nothing!

All of us have had that experience, I'm sure. We look around us and in total objectivity we see the solution, yet there is no obvious way for us to tell anyone. Try calling the traffic folks and saying, "I've got the answer to that bottleneck on the freeway." Or call the police department and tell whoever answers that you have a solution to a part of the crime problem. Of course, in both instances, whoever answers the phone will be polite, but probably also will be extremely condescending. Even if you happen to be friends with the person in charge, chances are your suggestions will go unheard or unheeded.

So what's the answer? Is it to sit in the traffic jam and gripe? Or should we just let the criminals walk over us? No. The answer is to speak out, to make phone calls, and to write letters. If you have the solution to the problem, speak out. The whole idea is to make your suggestion so palatable that you will be heard. And maybe, just maybe, your idea will be used and it will work. When is the last time you tried it?

Seeing the Good

When Florence Chadwick was attempting to swim from Catalina Island to Long Beach on one occasion, she had to quit. The combination of fog and fatigue was too much. When she realized how close she was to shore, she said, "I wouldn't have lost if I could have seen my goal."

That's a good line for most of us to remember. I could say it often! If only I could have seen all of my goals clearly, I would have achieved so much more.

One of the reasons we fail is because we neglect to make the goals clear enough. It's not the fog in the air which makes the goals hidden, it's the fact that they were cloudy in the first place. How long would we stay in business if we didn't establish some priorities for the year, and how long could we stay at work if we didn't check on those guidelines occasionally? A huge danger we face is to become so complacent in our work world that we get the false impression that renewed planning is not necessary.

The same principle holds in all aspects of life. As we grow older, we tend to think that we have seen it all and that our success simply comes naturally. That philosophy is dangerous of course, and once we stop planning ahead, as though we will live forever, we have lost an esssential spark of life.

If only the swimmer had kept going a little longer, the shoreline would have revealed itself through the fog. A little more perseverance and courage and planning will clear our goals too.

Pain, Stress, and Improvement

John Steinbeck wrote, "We have learned no technique, no ingredient that takes the place of anguish. If in some future mutation we are able to remove pain from our species, we will also remove genius and set ourselves closer to the mushroom."

When I first read the above quote, I chuckled a bit. I was younger then, and I didn't really think that we needed much pain or anguish to succeed. Now I have lived a little longer, and I think Mr. Steinbeck had a sound thought, even though I would rather never feel pain or anguish again.

I'm not sure just what kind of anguish the writer was thinking about, but I found comfort in the dictionary's definition of that word. According to Webster, anguish is extreme stress of body or mind. And who hasn't felt such pain at some time in the course of life?

Some of this type of stress is probably harmful and is the very thing which can cause mental or physical tragedies. A lot of this we permit ourselves to have, sometimes without realizing it, but the kind of anguish which causes us to realize that we haven't done the best can sometimes motivate us to do better. That's the kind of pain which is motivated by conscience, and perhaps that is what Steinbeck was considering. Take the pain-causing conscience from us, and we have indeed removed ourselves from the Power of Good in the universe.

We can do without pain to be sure, but we are dead when we have lost the incentive to improve.

Whoops!

Recently I sent a very good friend a birthday card in time for what I thought was his birthday. Somehow I had missed it by a month. I was early!

The next time I saw him he thanked me for the card and then kidded me about my premature greetings. The more he joked, the more I realized that I had made a grave error. In sending his card early, I had symbolically stolen a month from his life.

My friend is an old guy! Well, at least he's older than I am, so that gives him a certain amount of "old age." If he had been sixteen, he would have been thrilled that I had advanced his birth date. But there comes a time when we don't want to be older; we want to be younger. In each person that's a different age, but in the case of my friend, it is obvious that he already has reached it.

My first card was a mistake, innocently made. But I've been thinking a lot about the situation. I wonder if I've ever been guilty of acting older than I really am. I can remember times when my kids have said, "Dad, don't be such an old fuddy-duddy." And I can think of other times when I stubbornly held on to some belief, even when time had made that belief very old-fashioned. I even get in a rut sometimes by habits I've had too long and have failed to shake.

I'm going to send my friend another birthday card, and I hope that he will forgive me. I'm really sorry that I made him older than he is. He'll have enough trouble with growing older without my help.

INDEXES

Scriptural Cross Reference

Genesis
2:2 (work, Labor Day), 84
45:1 ff. (family, World War II,
  brothers), 100

Exodus
3:14 ("it"), 102
18:13-26 (jury duty, patriotism,
  citizenship), 58

Numbers
11:6 (lethargy, blahs), 95
13:33 (giants), 93

Deuteronomy
33:25b (honesty), 95

Joshua
1:8 (success), 78

I Samuel
17:1 (giants), 93

I Kings
19:9 ff. (storms of life), 20

116

117

Topical Index

121